RAISING CHILDREN

The greatest joy and most important responsibility you will ever have

OTHER BOOKS BY GARY W FRIENDSHUH

Stories For All Ages
Teach values while connecting and entertaining

A Path Less Taken: The True Life Adventures of One Man And His Faith Awakening
Life being an adventure, to be loved and be grateful for

A Path Less Taken: The True Life Adventures of Gary Friendshuh And His Faith Awakening
The immediate family version. A man's story should be passed on to his family, for a man's story is all he will truly ever own

All above available on Amazon.com or by contacting the author at gwfriendshuh@gmail.com (Love to hear your thoughts)

Little One & Other Children's Stories
Available at grandfathersstories.com

All profits for any of the above books will be donated to children's charities.

First U.S. Print Edition
Softcover ISBN: 978-1-945333-32-3
Hardcover ISBN: 978-1-945333-33-0
Library of Congress Control Number: 2024902288

All images used by permission.

Published in Rapid City, South Dakota, United States

RAISING CHILDREN

**The greatest joy and
most important responsibility
you will ever have**

as shared by a father, grandfather & great-grandfather

GARY W FRIENDSHUH

Dedication

Dedicated to Irene and Jeanne, who have
been wonderful mothers, and to my five
sons, my grandchildren, great-grandchildren,
and all the generations to come.

And to all the fathers taking on the most important
responsibility they will ever have, and to the
mothers who are encouraging and joining them.

May our Father in Heaven guide and bless you all.

Acknowledgments

Thanks to my loving, supportive wife Jeanne, and
to my sons Luke, Tim, Matt, Mark and Daniel,
without whom — and who they became — this
book could never have been written.

I also want to thank my good friend and editor
Barb Evenson for her invaluable help, and Kim Noce
and all the others who helped or encouraged me.

Contents

Introduction

This is one father's story. A story about raising four boys with my wife of twenty-four years and raising one more son by myself for close to seven years before remarrying.

Nothing I have ever done in my life is more important nor brought me more joy than raising my five sons. Hopefully my experiences, thoughts and lessons learned along the way may be of some help to fathers and mothers in raising their children.

Each of us have our own ideas of how to raise children and what we feel is important; but most of us are looking for input and suggestions. Where do we find that input today? In the 1800s, with no radio or television, people spent many hours visiting and sharing thoughts and ideas with one's parents, grandparents, extended family and friends. Sadly, very little of that sharing goes on today. Who then do we turn to? What do we choose to read?

I am a firm believer in education and all its contributions to mankind and society; yet I would rather hear from someone with hands-on experience and success than from learned educators, expounding theories based on other educational theories.

I believe our soft-handed, overly permissive society has caused many problems with several generations of children. As a rule, our society is too much into self, and raising children is about doing for another, even if it requires sacrifice of self. For me, part of that sacrifice of self was realizing I had a responsibility to my children and then trying to discover how best to fulfill that responsibility. One of the ways I took was to talk to people I trusted, people who had actually done a good job raising their children. I also read whatever I could get my hands on. But I didn't look for degrees and titles from those I chose to read, I looked for experience and results.

I looked at the generations before me and confirmed what our great-great grandfathers knew, our fathers should have known, and our society seems to have forgotten.

I do not believe how children turn out is an accident, nor is it just luck. It takes a lot of dedication and hard work and yes, sacrifice, but the rewards are as great as any reward could ever be.

My five adult sons are, by any set of standards, terrific human beings, and are my best friends. Raising my sons was the greatest joy in my life and not one of them ever rebelled or even talked back after the age of seven.

I have been so blessed in my life's journey that I try to not let a day go by without taking the time to thank the Lord. We all have been given gifts, and I have been given none greater than my boys. Wanting to give something back, I have tried to write a book that will help others experience the same joy. Hopefully, some of my children or my children's children or someone else may gain something from it.

Along with my personal experiences, I have included some advice. Sometimes that advice sounds more like orders than suggestions. I apologize for that. I do not mean to dictate or offend—I am not a writer, I am a father. I have tried to share some of the things that worked in raising my five sons. Please overlook the presentation, for there may be something here of value. Treat it like things your great great-grandfather may have heard or learned from his father or grandfather—not law, but helpful hints and lessons learned.

I will share something my oldest son wrote.

Ode to My Father

Written by Luke

As I struggle through parenthood I have come to appreciate more and more how well Dad raised us. I remember discussing with Tim how we never had the "need" to "fit in" and wondering where did that come from? Is it our innate independence or was it that we were so secure in who we were within our family—we already had somewhere we belonged and fit in—that we didn't need to find it outside of that? We decided it came from our family.

I think it is one of the things about my personality that I value most. Dad did such a good job of making us feel good about ourselves that we didn't need that support from anywhere else. I can only hope that I can get close to doing the same for my kids. It is a high standard I feel like I am not meeting much of the time.

Thank you Dad!

Thank you Luke—and you did a great job of raising your three sons!

On your journey through this book, you will get to know me a little. When you do, you may think I have raised my sons in an environment too out of the ordinary to have relevance for someone raising their children in what many might call a more normal set of circumstances. I honestly do not believe that to be the case. My friends and others I interviewed for this book encompassed many lifestyles and had a wide range of experiences. The things I talk about and the lessons I have learned can be applied in the suburbs, the city, the country, or anywhere.

It is true some environments are more challenging, but establishing good morals, close family ties, lack of peer pressure, a good work ethic and a sense of responsibility are important, no matter what environment you raise your children in.

I kept this book fairly short, with brief chapters for easy reference. Raising children is truly our greatest responsibility and perhaps there may be something here worth remembering.

I have also referred to all children as male for expediency. I believe what is shared here applies to girls as well as boys.

Within the text, I have included some poems, stories, and memories. Most are my own, but some are written by others.

I have been many things to many people on my life's journey, but I see myself first and foremost as a father.

I dedicate this book not only to my sons, but to fathers everywhere. I pray it may be of some value.

Children's children are the crown of old men;
And the glory of children are their fathers.
PROVERBS 17:6

My father holding me.

Tim, Matt, Mark, Luke

Daniel, me

Raising Children

The most important responsibility
we will ever have

When I take the time to reflect, I realize my sons are the most important responsibility I will ever have in my life. Our children are not only the future of our families, they are the future of our nation and of our world. How they are taught, the values they carry, and who they become will control what this nation and this world will be. From a family and spiritual sense, how could anything be more important than doing all we can to ensure our children become assets to society and our families, and are pleasing to God?

My wife and I did not believe it was enough to just love and care for our sons. We believed it was our responsibility to mold them into the kind of human beings we wished them to be. There was a price to pay, but the rewards for us and for our sons were immeasurable.

We soon realized the most difficult part of raising children is not the dirty diapers, the constant monitoring, the long hours, or even taking care of them when they are sick. It is requiring of ourselves whatever it takes to provide direction, values, discipline, guidance, truth, respect, responsibility, self-esteem and a good work ethic.

Almost all parents say they love their children, but some parents say children are so sweet until they become teenagers. Then they say "Look out!" Why? Because the teenage years were filled with rebellion, hurt, and worry.

Perhaps the teenage years were so difficult because those parents didn't take on their responsibility in the preteen years. We paid a small price early, and our teenage sons were a wonderful joy in our life. We could not have started when our sons were teenagers. We needed to start when they were very young.

I have always believed whatever a child learns in his first five years, whether taught intentionally or picked up on his own, will stay with him forever. I also believe the first three years are the most important of the five. We felt our responsibility began at conception and lasted until our child was an adult, but the most important time of all was our child's first three years.

Most of us get so busy with our lives that it takes a conscious effort to go beyond just living our lives and loving our children. When a child is less than three, it is especially easy to just live and love, and not face the fact that we should require so much more of ourselves.

My wife and I realized that how we chose to interact with our very young son would have a profound effect on him for the rest of his life. We knew how important our being there was. Touching, snuggling, and talking to our son was not just loving him. It was training him and fulfilling part of his basic needs.

When our first son was born, I felt like I loved him so much I could hardly stand it. I can even remember being afraid I might hurt him, because he was so little and I wanted to hug him so much. Without a doubt, most of us love our children in this way. We would do anything for them, including give our very life for them. Yet I realized that if I acted like a lot of modern day fathers I would not have been giving my son what he was entitled to.

It is so easy to look the other way. It is much easier to do it for our young son than to make him do it. It is simpler to pick up our son's toys rather than to make him do it. It is quicker to do family chores ourselves rather than to make our son do them. And when our son throws a fit or won't do what he is told, it is so tempting to ignore him or look the other way.

Besides, it hurts our heart to have to come down on him. It hurts worse to have to punish him. The same father who would think nothing of grabbing a red-hot car door on a burning vehicle to get his son out often won't even endure a little heartache for the same child. If we take the easy route, if we look the other way, if we don't train and discipline our son, we are depriving him of that which he is entitled to; and the lack of discipline is not his fault. It is our fault. The fact we may later be hurt by this lack of discipline was our choice, but he will be hurt too; and that is not his choice, but ours! The longer we wait, the more difficult the job.

A lot of people wait too long. We formed bonds with our sons early. We gave them a strong sense of family and of self. We started training and disciplining them as young children.

As they got older, we would no longer have been willing to put up with unacceptable behavior, because they were old enough to know better. Wrong! They only knew better because we taught them to know better; if we had not taken the difficult route of teaching them what they should know while young, the more difficult it would have been. Most children will not accept discipline for the first time as teenagers, so they rebel and the battle is on. If the love is there and shown, in the end all will probably turn out okay; but you will be saying, as most of modern day parents say, "Raising teenagers was horrible."

My grandparents never had trouble with the teenage years of my father's generation. The kids just did what they were told. But in those years parents didn't have to deal with peer pressure, television, computers, cell phones, lots of bad examples and a society that gives out wrong messages. In a way, they had it easy.

It was more difficult for my wife and I, but we took the good from past generations and taught our sons when they were very young before outside influences were part of their lives.

Walk A Little Plainer, Daddy

Author unknown

Walk a little plainer, Daddy,
Said a little boy so frail.
I'm following in your footsteps,
And I don't want to fail.

Sometimes your steps are very plain,
Sometimes they are hard to see,
So walk a little plainer Daddy,
For you are leading me.

I know that once you walked this way
Many years ago,
And what you did along the way,
I'd really like to know.

For sometimes when I am tempted,
I don't know what to do.
So walk a little plainer, Daddy,
For I must follow you.

Someday when I'm grown up,
You are like I want to be.
Then I will have a little boy,
Who will want to follow me.

And I would want to lead him right,
And help him to be true.
So walk a little plainer, Daddy,
For we must follow you.

Bumper car

In the Womb

When my wife was pregnant with our first son, he was quiet and very calm in her womb. Our second son rolled and kicked, and was very active. Because her second pregnancy was so different from her first, she thought surely this meant the child must be a girl.

Instead, our second son was born, and he was truly different from our first. At a year old you could take our first born, Luke, set him on a dock and he would just sit there, or perhaps stick his finger in the water. Our second son, Tim, on the same dock, would run off it, and plunge into the lake without a second thought.

Luke played quietly on the kitchen floor, while Tim was always banging or throwing something and making loud sounds of delight or anger. We used to call him "Bumper Car" because he would bump his walker into anything and everything. He went off the stairs without even slowing down. We put a chair in front of the stairs. He moved the chair, and once again went head over heels down the stairway. We put a gate on top of the stairs. He tore the gate down and went head over heels a third time. We finally put in a very heavy-duty gate that kept him from a fourth fall.

Our two sons' personalities and respective natures were obviously there, even in their mother's womb.

There is no way we could have raised the two of them exactly the same way. Each had their own unique temperament and personality, yet both of them needed lots and lots of love and care, and that began when they were still in the womb.

How I treated my pregnant wife, and for that matter how she treated herself, was a reflection of how the both of us were treating our unborn child within her. Our son felt his mother's emotions, became familiar with her voice and the voices of those close to her, particularly mine.

We began outwardly showing our love for our son, even before he was born. I took the time to lie with my wife and talk lovingly with her and towards our son. I did not allow myself to yell or raise my voice at her during her pregnancy. She could not leave our son in the other room and I knew I would be yelling and raising my voice at him too. We certainly had our disagreements during her pregnancy. But I could not imagine what she was going through, so I felt I could go through a little difficulty of my own by doing whatever it took to keep things on an even keel. As the father, I tried to make sure I never got angry at her in front of my son—either before or after he was born.

Some modern psychologists claim children should see their parents angry with one another, so they learn conflict is a part of life. I strongly disagree. A young child needs security second only to needing love; and the younger the child, the more incapable he is of understanding that Mom and Dad fighting is no big deal.

We kept our disagreements to ourselves, had our arguments behind closed doors, and gave our sons the security of a united mother and father. One of the greatest gifts a father can give his children is to love their mother. Children will learn soon enough that there is conflict in the world, and they will learn how to deal with it.

We did not give our sons any insecurity by allowing them to see or feel conflict between their mother and me—even when they were in the womb. A child will feel anything his mother feels; if she feels anger, sorrow, or fear, so will he. He won't know what it is, but he will feel it, and it won't feel good.

Science has proven that a child even recognizes his father's voice before he is born. It stands to reason that a soft, loving tone will affect him very differently than a harsh or angry tone; and the more he hears his dad's voice, the more comfortable he will be with it. So we allowed our son to get to know me, even before he had seen the light of day.

Let Me Out of Here!

Just before Tim was born, mom brought Luke, who was about fifteen months old, into her bed and had him put his hand on her tummy. So close to his due date, Tim was especially anxious to get out of his confined quarters and was kicking up a storm. Even dad, who joined the family get-together on the bed, was surprised at all the movement. I didn't even have to put my hand on her belly to feel it, I could actually see it! When Luke had his hand on her tummy, we told him the movement he felt was his new baby brother or sister wanting to come out and meet him. I don't know how to describe the look on his face. All I can think of is a combination of excitement, wonder, astonishment, and joy. God's miracle.

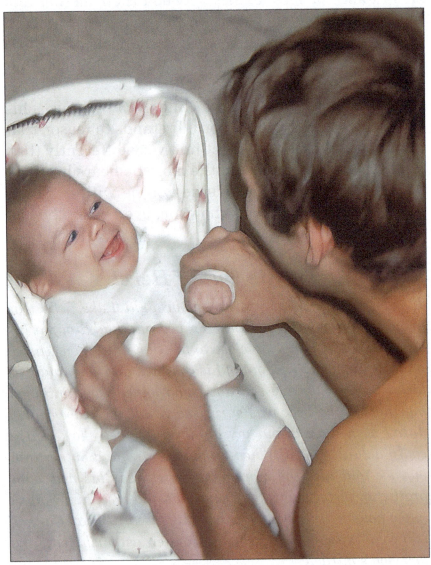

Matt and Dad

Mom and Dad

Do they have different roles?

A child is truly blessed if he has both a mother and a father to help raise him. A parent, too, is blessed to have a husband or wife by their side helping raise their children.

I have learned so much over the years about being both mom and dad. As a general rule, I believe God has given most people special gifts and abilities that are generally attributed to their particular sex; but our gifts, needs, wants, and desires should not be limited by our sex.

Parents should discover between them where their individual strengths and weaknesses are, and help each other as a team. It does not matter which parenting jobs either of them fulfills, as long as those jobs are done. In our particular case, we chose traditional roles. The children went more to their mother to be hugged and snuggled, and to have their cuts and bruises taken care of. They learned not to cry unnecessarily, and looked to their father more as the authoritarian in the family.

With my fifth son, who I raised on my own from age one to age seven, I found out how difficult it was to play both roles. I wanted my young son to come crying to me when he was hurt and get a special hug. Yet I also wanted to teach him to cowboy up, stop crying, and learn to be tough. It was a difficult double role.

It is always important to be ourselves, the self that we are proud of. However even in a two-parent family that can present a problem. For example, if my wife and I both had very mild natures, perhaps neither of us would want to discipline or administer tough love. In that case, one or both of us would have to step outside our nature and take on that uncomfortable responsibility. Even though most would not think of me as mild-mannered, I found it difficult to discipline my sons. I did it though, because my father taught me that it was the right thing to do, and because he taught me that a father must do what has to be done.

Even though my wife and I had strengths that the other lacked, there were times when one or the other of us had to step outside our natures. There were times when she was not up to giving hugs or extra love and I had to step in. At times, particularly when I was not around, she had to do a lot of disciplining. Here is where having two parents was really a benefit. One of us could take care of a difficult situation one time and the other at another time. Don't get me wrong—we did not feel like we had to stick to any particular role as long as one of us was doing what our sons needed. And we knew those needs required not only a parent's time but a parent's discipline.

One of the best and most necessary things we did was to set aside some time each day, or at absolute minimum once a week. We both took time from our hectic schedules to talk at length about our sons and how things were going. We shared particular views, thoughts, and fears with each other. We discussed what perhaps one or both of us could do to help the other with a particular problem, or to help a particular boy with a special need, problem, or fear. The years spent raising my fifth son Daniel alone were very different. I really missed not having someone there who knew and loved Daniel as much as I did, to talk things over with.

The older four boys' mother and I talked all the time about how we thought the boys were doing. Sometimes we would agree that one of them needed extra love and attention, and then we would remind and help each other work on that. We did not keep things to ourselves. We talked often about the boys; we shared our joy, pain, and views with each other, and our sons benefited greatly.

To fathers out there who are a part of a two-parent family, I would like to encourage you not to miss out. You will never have this time with your son again. I missed a lot with my older four boys before they were a year old. Having just started a business, I was busy working, and at that time, felt like it was more mom's job to take care of an infant. I didn't realize how much I'd missed. Luckily, I was blessed with a fifth son and was able to share in his complete development. Learning to deal with an infant was an irreplaceable joy, and it made me realize what I had missed with the other four.

As a new father, if you are not immediately comfortable with an infant, I suggest you keep trying. Hopefully you will learn to be comfortable and to look forward to more extended time with your son.

No one else can assume the parent's role, unless a parent is blessed enough to have a good grandmother or grandfather present. If at all possible, one of the parents should stay home with their child until he is at least three years old. If that is absolutely not possible, make it for as long as you can. Six weeks is better than five or whatever you can make work. When parents absolutely can't have one of them stay at home, they will just have to spend as much time as possible with their child when they are there, even at the expense of other things in their lives.

Instead of giving parents tax credits for daycare, I wish our government gave tax credits to the family who chooses to have one parent stay at home with the children during these most important formative years.

Absolutely nothing money can buy will do as much for a child as one parent being there. Oh, how I wish parents would think about this, and ask themselves whether anyone else can truly do what is required for their child. I strongly believe the answer is "No!" Every child needs lots and lots of touching, cuddling, hugging, and attention—way beyond what a non-relative or group caregiver is capable of giving.

It has been shown through generations of good families, and substantiated through scientific research, that the first three years of a child's life are the most important. Over 90% of our brain development occurs prior to age three, and that development, both intellectual and emotional, is directly affected by the amount of intimacy a child experiences during that time. Loving, touching, hugging, and talking to a young child are all infinitely important, and no non-parent can give what a parent can.

If after the first three years both parents are working, then they will have to decide between them who takes on what responsibilities.

In a traditional family a father works hard and may be under a lot of pressure. But he will not experience any more pressure than a mother experiences when her child is sick, and when she might also feel under the weather. Add to that the fact that she hasn't had a good night's sleep in a long time and perhaps was even up most of the night before, and she truly is under a lot of pressure. Even when the children are not sick or particularly troublesome, she needs to have some relief. It should not matter how tired and exhausted a father is—he needs to give her some time every day. It does not have to be all at one time, but she may need to get away and just have some time to herself.

If the traditional male and female roles have been reversed, then, hopefully, mom will also relieve dad in the same manner.

Lastly, I do not know what to say to a working mother or father raising their children alone. If the absent parent is in the child's life, I have some experience with this. I talk about it in the chapter, "Raising My Child Alone." If the other parent is not around or is unwilling to help, hopefully grandparents, other family members, or a good friend can be there. If none of that is available, look for the smallest day care you can afford. And may our Lord help and guide you.

Dog

When Luke was in the second grade, Tim in first, and Matt in kindergarten, they used to walk about a quarter of a mile through the woods to catch the bus. They had a little log cabin at the end of the driveway they could wait in.

Our dog, named Dog, would go with them to the bus and then come home after they got picked up. One morning, Dog didn't come home; and when I left for work, I found him dead in the ditch by the little log cabin.

When the boys got home that evening, we asked them what had happened.

They said Dog was on the other side of the road when the milk truck came along. He was running back towards them, and got hit by the truck.

They said that it took all three of them to be able to drag him off the road, and then the bus came and they got on.

Their mother and I just looked at each other. Then she asked, "Didn't it bother you?"

Luke said, "I found it really hard not to cry."

Postscript

That night, their mother and I talked about the whole incident. She thought they were a little too tough for their young ages. I was proud.

We were probably both right.

The First Six Weeks

A child needs lots of love and physical contact during his first six weeks. If mom is nursing, he will get a lot of physical contact. If mom chooses not to nurse or is unable to nurse, then hopefully she will set aside a lot of time when she can hold and snuggle with him. A child cannot get too much physical contact. And he needs it from his father too. If mother is unable to give him lots and lots of it, then father will just have to give him even more.

All the books that proclaim so many benefits for a child because of nursing are correct, not just because of the milk that comes from mom, but because of all the touching, contact, and closeness given to a nursing child. Most moms just naturally know it is important to talk to their son as they are nursing, and they talk in a loving, soothing manner. I, as a dad, did this too. I talked to my infant son as often as I could. According to studies, the more words a child hears from a loving parent prior to age three, the better his intellectual development will be.

I talked to our son often—I didn't leave it all to mom. We talked normally and did not use baby talk. We were amazed at how quickly our son learned and grew to understand. It is a good habit to get into early, the habit of talking normally rather than in baby talk, because he will understand before anyone is even aware of it.

My wife and I found it very hard to let our infant son cry. When he was crying we tried to make sure he was not hungry, hurting, afraid, or uncomfortable. With a small infant, it is very difficult to tell if he has a tummy ache or needs burping. But we soon recognized his cries. There were soft cries we learned were not out of fear or discomfort. He may have just been exercising his lungs. Yes, there were cries of anger, of hurt, and even "I am here" cries and "I want to be held" cries.

If a parent is very lucky, he or she may even have a child like our number three son, Matt, who almost never cried and always seemed happy and cooing. I personally believe that during the first six weeks you cannot give too much attention or love, so if mom can't be there, father should be. If we were to error, we wanted it to be on the side of giving too much attention. But before they began crawling, our sons were trained to know that they couldn't be picked up whenever they cried. Demands on parents' time and of everyday living will dictate that parents do some of this training without even being aware of it.

Too Cute to Handle

When I got home from work, I would first kiss my wife, and then I looked in on Luke. I could not get over how tiny he was. He seemed too small to be real.

After my shower and looking in on him again, I would anxiously wait for him to wake up. In the beginning, he seemed to be sleeping all the time, except through the night, that is (smile).

When I heard him making sounds, I would go in and look at him through his mobile. As soon as he was able to see, whenever I walked into the room and looked down at him, he broke into a wide grin. His mouth was wide open, and he would kick his feet and shake his arms. He knew his daddy!

At first, when I picked him up, I had to be very careful to support his neck; but soon he became strong enough to support it himself. He even developed a tight grip. He liked squeezing my finger, and he loved pulling my hair. It hurt!

I loved him so much and loved hugging him so much that I was afraid I would squeeze too hard. I cannot tell you the joy he brought into my life. ...

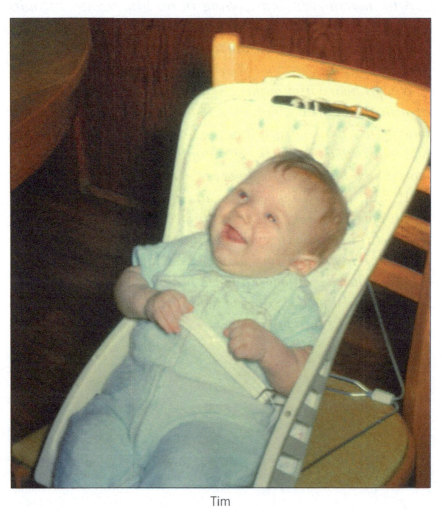

Tim

Six Weeks to Crawling

Children learn to roll over, crawl, walk, talk, and mind at their own pace and in their own time frame. There are no magic dates, numbers, or ages. Each child is different, unique unto himself, and even children in the same family will progress at different rates. Some will sleep more, laugh more, or cry more.

As we got to know our son and he got to know us, we showed him he was important, and that we were going to be there for him—be there with lots and lots of love, cuddling, and soft loving talk. But some time before he began crawling, we believed it was best for him to learn he could not be picked up every time he cried. We decided based on what we'd learned about his different cries.

Luke also helped me recognize the importance of holding, touching, and showing lots of affection. When he was about five months old, he didn't seem to be able to roll over. We found out he had a congenital hip condition. He had to be put in a brace. His legs were spread like a frog, and he couldn't move them. Talk about breaking our hearts—our poor little first-born baby boy. Yet perhaps the brace did something besides

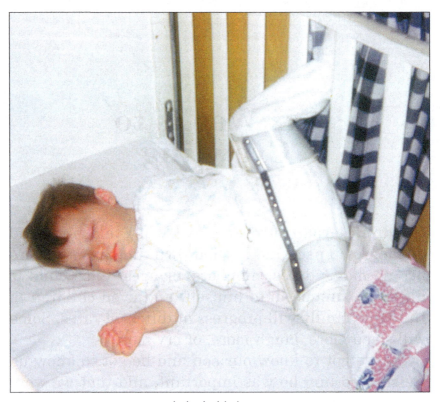

Luke in his brace

correct a physical defect. It made us be so much more attentive to him. We held him more, cuddled with him more, and scratched under the brace for hours. Thus, we developed this habit of closeness we carried over to our other sons, so perhaps it was a blessing in disguise.

Another important habit is having a bedtime routine. Young children and toddlers are not being naughty when they struggle or cry when being put to bed or trying to get back to sleep. The key is to help them feel safe and feel their parent's presence even when they are not there! Put them to bed with a routine and reassure them. Even though they may be too young to understand the words, every night say to them, "I always come and check on you. Mommy or Daddy is always looking after you. Here, I will pull the cover over you to keep you warm and cozy. We will always be looking in on you."

The routine is what is important. An infant or a toddler loves familiarity and patterns so the more consistently this routine is used, the more the infant or toddler will recognize it and feel safe and ready for sleep. Even a song can be part of a bedtime routine as the following story illustrates.

Sixteen Tons

One time when Mark was home visiting from college, I left him to watch Daniel while I went to town.

Daniel was about a year old and was asleep when I left.

I think he was cutting teeth or something, because when he woke up, Mark could not get him to stop crying.

Then Mark remembered he had seen and heard me singing to Daniel many times, so he tried.

He walked back and forth with the baby on his shoulder, patting his back and trying to sing him back to sleep.

Nothing seemed to work, and Mark was getting really frustrated. Then he remembered the song he had most often heard me sing.

In as deep a voice as he could muster, he started singing "Sixteen Tons."

Daniel went right back to sleep. Go figure?

Crawling to Walking

When our son began to crawl and before he learned to walk, we taught him the word "No." He needed to be taught for his own safety and protection and as the foundation for his future development. Our work truly began here. It would have been so much easier to overlook, allow, or even view as cute his minor disobedience or stubbornness at this early age. It would have been very easy to overlook things, and to avoid the difficult challenge of correction even for the next few years. But there would have come a time when we would no longer be willing to allow him to be disobedient; and if we hadn't laid the early foundation, we would have had a very difficult time teaching him when he got older.

A noted physician and child psychologist wrote a book on childcare, and most of her ideas were of great value to me. Yet I would love to talk with her about one of the things she said. She said never to match wills with a one-year-old because you could not win. How wrong she was! If you cannot match wills with a one-year-old and win, how are you going to be able to match wills with a thirteen-year-old and win? As difficult as it seemed at the time, it was insignificant compared to the difficulty we would have had with our teenagers if we had not won the early battles. We had all the advantages at this early age. We chose our battles carefully, picking only those we were willing to pursue to the end, and then made sure we did win.

Some people are not comfortable calling them battles. "Challenges" is perhaps a better word. But whatever we choose to call them, they are truly there. With my easy-going first son, Luke, a harsh "No" was all it took to stop him from doing whatever he was doing. This was more like a challenge. With my number two son, Tim, and his personality, he challenged me before he was even out of his walker, and continued to challenge me for several years.

Tim's personality required much more monitoring, but that monitoring paid enormous benefits in the long run. He learned, just as his brothers learned; and he learned very young, when we had the advantages and control.

We paid the price at this early age, and by the time our sons reached the age of seven, we had it made. Sure, we had minor confrontations after that age; but they were truly minor, because all the ground rules and foundations had been established. With Tim's personality, establishing my authority at age one was essential and more easily reinforced at age two, three and beyond. By the time Tim was seven, he knew and accepted my authority; and the rest was easy.

All human beings are given a free will and even a very young child wants to do things his way. When a child wants to play with a knife, parents have no trouble saying "No" and not allowing him to have his way. No matter what kind of fuss he throws, parents won't let him play with a sharp knife. No one has to tell parents to take it away because it is obvious he could get hurt.

But my wife and I understood our son could get hurt, perhaps just as seriously, by not teaching him he must obey us or those who are in authority. Taking the knife away was easy, yet making him come to the table or pick up his toys when he threw a fit was difficult. We realized that, at some point, getting his way could be just as harmful to him as playing with knives.

I know a family with parents who tried to do everything right. They were both teachers at a private school. He was also the principal, and she stayed home with their two girls until they started school. They taught their children good values, and their girls turned out to be very fine adults. Yet when I interviewed them about raising children, they said there was no way they would want to do that again. They were not willing to put up with all the stress of having teenagers.

I asked them to give me some examples of the stressful stuff. They had good kids, but in every example, their girls wanted things their own way. For instance, every Sunday morning a big fight developed because their daughters didn't want to wear outfits the parents thought were appropriate for church. A big argument seemed to start whenever the girls were told to do something. The parents were caught in the trap many parents fall into. They did not allow their girls to play with knives, but they allowed their girls to have too much freedom in other areas.

While they did not teach them to submit to their parent's authority, they did teach them to submit to other authorities, such as their teachers. But the girls were unwittingly taught that if they put up enough of a fuss, they didn't have to do what their parents told them. The parents didn't do this on purpose. The teachers wouldn't put up with any fuss and the girls knew it, so they did what they were told. The parents, on the other hand, loved the girls so much and they disliked forcing them to do what they were told. They were moved by a sad face or hurt look, or sometimes impressed, by their daughters' spirit, independence, or strong will.

At the time, it didn't seem like such a bad thing if the girls refused to come to the dinner table when they were told, or refused to pick up their toys. They mostly did what they were told; and it was much easier to let them do it later in their own time, or worse yet, to do it for them because they loved them so much. At first, it was just not coming to dinner once in a while. Then it was an occasional hassle about not going to bed; and in both cases, the parents could coax or talk the girls into it. When the girls were very young, mom or dad could almost always talk them into doing what they were asked to do; and this seemed like such a loving and thoughtful way to do it. WRONG!

As the girls got a little older, they were less likely to be talked into doing what they didn't want to do, and so they were allowed to have their own way more often. The girls weren't taught that they had to do what mom and dad told them to do, just because they were told to do it. The precedent was set, and when the girls became teenagers, they wanted things their own way more. They no longer could be talked into doing it the parents' way. During their younger years, the parents had been the nice guys. They tried to persuade their girls to do as they asked, and it seemed to work most of the time.

Eventually the girls could no longer be persuaded, and the battle was on. It seemed like every time the girls were told to do something, a fight developed. Aside from this mistake, these parents did almost everything else right. The worst harm to come of these battles was the parents' misery during their daughters' teenage years. As a result, they would never want to raise teenagers again.

For those of us who make many more mistakes in many other areas, the harm could be much more serious. Teenagers do not have well-developed judgment and life experience, and their decisions can be negatively influenced by peer pressure or hormones. If they do not follow parents' guidelines or orders, but continue to do things their own way during their teenage years, they can make wrong, even dangerous, choices. Those wrong choices could possibly ruin the rest of their lives, or even result in their death. Why put those we love at such risk, when we can avoid that risk by doing the difficult thing in the beginning? It is difficult to make those we love so much do what they are told; especially when at the time what they were told doesn't seem so important. It is extremely important! We must teach our children that they have to do what they are told just because we told them to do it. Period!

If your one-year-old is taught that he must do what

he is told every time, and it is reinforced when he is two, three, and right on up the ladder, parenting will get easier as he gets older—not harder. Yes, he will continually test us; but when we continue to meet that test head on, he will back right off. By the time he is a teen, he will have learned. He will know he must do it our way, and that will be that. We will have helped protect him from his own possible youthful foolishness, and we will have allowed his teenage years to be safer and more of a joy for both him and his parents.

Once he gets into school and around others who are being raised very differently, he will want to do what everyone else seems to do. He has to have a solid foundation to withstand peer pressure or the so-called modern way of thinking. He has to have pride in his family, and pride in himself. He needs to know what is expected of him in his family and that we all take pride in the way our family does things.

When I required my sons to do what they were told, I always tried to praise them for doing it; even if it had required a lot of effort on my part to get them to do it. I acted as though they had obeyed readily, and praised them for being such super kids. Human nature being what it is, they didn't remember the hassle. They just remembered the praise and were proud of themselves because I was proud of them.

Having said all that, we remembered to allow our infant to be an infant. We didn't get angry when he spit his food, or refused to eat, or when he threw it at us. Life should be a joy; and we realized that having a baby around will mean having lots of messes to clean up, and lots of things broken. The baby really knows no better, and at one time we too thought it was fun to see something fall on the floor and break.

We taught our son slowly and gently what he was capable of learning. We started with the word "No," but didn't use it all the time. We used it sparingly at first, and with regards to only one or two things until we knew he understood it. We did not try to force our son to eat, or lose patience with him when he spilled or got dirty, at this early stage. We felt it was enough he learned the word "No," and that he learned he couldn't always be picked up or have his own way. If we had used the word "No" every time he did something wrong, we would have been using it all the time.

We wanted our son to grow up feeling good about himself. If he did twenty-five things wrong and one thing right, we praised him for the one right thing. We did train him not to do the wrong things, but ever so slowly. For every time he heard the word "No," we found something to praise him for, four-fold. When he started to do more things right, it was easier to praise him even more. Then we slipped in "No" more often. The "No" seemed insignificant compared to all the positive reinforcement.

A Calf, a Walker, and a Finger

When Daniel was a baby, I built an elevated car seat so he could see out the window as we drove over the ranch.

When he was very young, the jostling of the pickup would almost always put him to sleep.

As we got into the cow herd, usually the mooing of the cattle would wake him. He would get very excited around the cows, and giggle with delight when a young calf charged the truck. His first word was cow, and I was there to hear it.

One cold morning, I found a newborn calf closer to dead than alive. I picked him up and put him on the floorboard of the truck, just below Daniel. We brought him back to the house and put him in an empty stock tank on the kitchen floor.

Daniel was running around in his walker at the time and was constantly running over to the stock tank and looking in. Soon the calf was standing on his feet and always looking for a bottle to suck.

The next thing I knew, Daniel was petting him with one hand, and the calf was sucking one of his fingers.

Doctoring calves like this happened frequently, and Daniel was used to seeing me help and save calves. If a calf was dead, I was careful not to let him see it. When he got a little older, he did notice I had thrown a dead calf on the back of the truck. When I got back into the pickup, he asked me, "Daddy, make it better?"

Moments like these made all the dirty diapers and the waking up at night worth every bit of the effort.

Postscript

Dads, you can take your very young son with you too, even if it is just to the mailbox or to the store. Do it whenever you can. The moments of joy and wonder will far outweigh the extra effort.

Potty ~~Training~~
Encouraging

The reason I crossed out "training" and put in "encouraging" is because we learned there should be little or no training here. Yes, we bought a child's potty and encouraged him to use it but we made sure it was one hundred percent encouragement and not training.

Most children have been trained, but there are children who are physically incapable of controlling their bodily functions until they have matured a little.

We let nature take its course. We did not try to enforce it or even strongly encourage it.

I actually think some children sleep too soundly to wake up and go to the bathroom. Perhaps there are even some nerves in the body related to letting a child know he has to go or allowing him to hold it back a little, and in some children, those nerves develop later in life.

One of the most manly men I have ever known wet his bed at night until he was almost twelve years old. And he was a child who worked like a man before he learned to sleep through the night without wetting.

I really believe it was something physical that he had no control over. One of my sons had a similar issue.

If any child falls into that category he may have a lot of difficulty maintaining his self-esteem. He will likely think badly of himself, but it is up to his parents to let him know it is not his fault. It is a physical thing.

We got a bed pad, and let him know he was not in trouble and we assured him he will be able to control it when his nerves fully develop.

I know a set of parents who forced their child to sit on the potty for extended times. That child had some serious physical issues, to say nothing of the mental and self-esteem issues.

Most everyone needs to be relaxed in order to let nature take its course, and a young child will have a lot of trouble relaxing if he thinks he is being forced to do something, or if he thinks there is something wrong with him because he is having trouble.

Let nature take its course!

Working with Nature

My fifth son, Daniel, was born at home. I got to be in the delivery room when my other four sons were born but being at home was much different and very special. We had a midwife there and everything went naturally but we were prepared to go to the hospital in case there were any problems.

Going to the hospital can present some problems even if you have no intention of having the child at home. My oldest son, Luke, and his wife, Carolyn, were about to have their third child. On their way to the hospital, nature had other plans. Their son Tristan was born in the van on the way there. Everything turned out okay but it made all the papers.

Luke's son Jordan and his wife, Opal, planned to have their first child at home but were prepared to go to the hospital if there were any problems.

After many hours of labor, the midwife told them it was time to go to the hospital, and they did just that. An ultrasound showed the baby in a horizontal position and seemingly stuck so they had no alternative but to perform a c-section. All turned out just fine but it really illustrates how important being prepared is.

Nature does things on her own terms.

Dad, Luke and Tim

Should I discipline

Parents absolutely should discipline! Choosing how to discipline is a personal decision. I chose to tap my boys on their bottoms or to tap their hands, and yet I know parents who never tapped their children at all. Some would give timeouts, where the child was forced to sit on a chair for a period of time as a punishment. I personally think this type of discipline may work with some children, but I doubt it would have worked with a child such as my number two son. He had such a strong personality right from the get-go; I am not sure he would have stayed on the chair even at age one or two.

A very young child may not even understand a timeout, but he immediately understands a tap on the butt or hand. I called these TLTs for Tender Love Taps. With such a definite, quick response as a tap on the behind, you can follow up more quickly with love and reassurance. Any form of punishment must be followed with love and reassurance. Depending on the child's age and what he did wrong, the love and reassurance should almost be overwhelming.

We wanted our son to come away from the whole experience with a sense of feeling loved and feeling good about himself. Even if our son was too young to understand what we were saying, we talked comfortingly and reassuringly about what just happened. We felt we were building the foundation for future talks that would be understood and hopefully absorbed.

The younger the child, the more quickly he will need this comfort, reassurance, and love after the TLT. With our one-year-old, we started comforting him within ten seconds of the TLT. But even with our five-year-old, the comforting started within a few minutes. With a child of perhaps seven years old, some may choose to allow him to stew a little before comforting him, but not very long. Remember, a child needs the TLT, but he needs to feel good about himself even more. When a child is three or four, he might even need a CLS (Controlled Love Swat)—only on the bottom, of course.

One of the reasons I prefer a TLT over a timeout is because he is punished immediately, and very soon thereafter he is hugged, loved and made to feel good about himself. The punishment is quickly over, and he has very little time to think of himself as a bad boy. If he sits in a corner for five or ten minutes, he has those five or ten minutes to think of himself as a bad boy. I don't like that at all.

Using TLTs also allowed us to begin training our son more effectively at a younger age. It does you no good to take the knickknack off the coffee table or to take a one-year-old away from the knickknack. He must learn not to touch it.

When my number two son, Tim, was around a year old he was in his walker, came up to the coffee table, and put his hand on a knickknack. I said "No" and he pulled his hand away and looked at me. He then reached up again, and I said "No" more harshly and loudly. Once again, he pulled his hand away. Then he reached out for a third time. I said "No" and gently slapped his hand with two fingers. He pouted, looked at me, and reached out again. I slapped his hand a little harder. I was amazed when, with tears in his eyes, he reached out yet again. This time I stung his hand.

He cried loudly, but did not reach out any more. This truly was more difficult for me and seemed more like a miniature battle than a challenge. It truly hurt me more than it did him; but I had to do what was necessary, even if it was very difficult. Tim's personality required much more monitoring, but it paid enormous benefits in the long run. He learned, just as his brothers learned; and he learned very young, when I had all the advantages and control.

Tim's actions at age one showed me how strong a will even a one-year-old can have. I personally believe a strong will is not a bad trait, but it sure will make a parent's job more difficult. A child with a strong will has to learn he can't always have his way, both now and throughout his life; and a parent needs to teach him that. He needs to learn he must do things just because his parents tell him to. Period. The end! The younger he is taught the easier it is going to be, both for his parents and for him.

It may or may not do any good to put a one-year-old in a chair because he touched a knick-knack after he was told not to, but the same one-year-old certainly will immediately understand a tap on the hand after you have told him "No." As a child matures, some may then choose a CLS or even use something like a timeout.

Hopefully, everyone should be able to dispense with CLSs by the time a child is nine or ten. If the price has been paid in the formative years, none should be necessary at that late age.

I have had child psychologists tell me spankings are wrong. They like to refer to a parent spanking his child as a parent hitting a child. They say no child deserves to be hit. I agree, we should never hit a child. Now, we are talking about a definition. I do not believe tapping your child's hands with two fingers or even swatting his bottom with an open hand is hitting—even if it does sting. No one should ever hit a child, and a TLT should only be administered on the hands and a CLS on the bottom. They are appropriate when followed with lots and lots of love and affection.

We did not listen to our overly permissive society. We raised our sons closer to the way our great-great grandparents raised theirs. Then, reasonable discipline was not only accepted, but almost all parents recognized it as the correct and right thing to do.

The School Bus

Daniel went to a private grade school, but he rode the public school bus.

It was the only bus in the entire district which was forever having discipline problems. The problems got so out of hand that the school threatened to discontinue running that particular bus route.

A couple of other parents and I jumped into action and organized a meeting between the parents of the children on that bus, the school principal, and the bus manager.

We discovered only four or five kids caused all the

problems. I suggested a child be given a warning each time he got into trouble, and that parents had to sign each warning. After three warnings, the child would be kicked off the bus for a month. If he got in trouble again, he would be kicked off the bus for the balance of the year.

I was shocked and amazed when one of the parents said the warnings wouldn't do any good. She felt it was the school's responsibility to give them detention or some other form of punishment. She further stated her son would consider it a badge of honor to get kicked off the bus so that wouldn't do any good either.

I said, "Sorry, ma'am, but I don't think it is the school's responsibility to discipline your children. It is yours; and if getting kicked off the bus doesn't do your son any good, at least the rest of the children won't have to put up with him anymore." I do not remember her response. She may have even walked out, but the warning system was approved.

About three weeks later, Daniel got a warning! I didn't find it until after he left for school the next day.

That afternoon, I picked Daniel up after school and asked him to tell me about the warning. He told me he was standing up when the bus was moving and the bus driver told him to sit down and stay sitting. Instead, later he forgot and stood up again.

We talked about it a little, and I told him as a fourth grader, he should know better. Then I asked him if he knew how to walk through town to get to Highway 385, just west of the ranch. He said he did.

I told him he wouldn't have to walk through town this time, but riding the bus was a privilege, and if he wasn't allowed to ride the bus, he might have to walk to and from school.

By road it is fourteen miles to school, but over the mountain it is only about three and a half or four miles. I then drove him to the spot on the highway just west of the ranch and told him I wanted him to know what it would be like to have to walk.

I told him to get out and walk home.

It was over a three-mile walk through rough country, up and down a mountain, with no roads, no homes, and lots of wildlife. Daniel's older brother had tried to come in from the west side more than once, and each time he had gotten lost. He had to call for directions on his cell phone, or turn around; but he wasn't raised here.

When I left Daniel off, he knew Jeanne was with me. What he didn't know was I brought her along so I could have a little insurance (I needed her to drive the car home). When Daniel got out of sight, I got out with my binoculars, and followed him at a distance.

He did a terrific job. He did get a little mixed up and added about a quarter of a mile to his walk, but he came through the cow herd, jumped several small herds of deer, and did just fine. I even watched him get a drink at the well, sit down on a rock, and watch an eagle soar overhead.

When he finally got home, he was mad and upset, but Jeanne had a talk with him. She said he should be proud of himself for making such a long walk through rough country. He then was proud, but more importantly, he never got into trouble on the bus again.

Disciplining
in Public

When Tim was between two and three, we had a talk about being good before we went to church. Once we were there, he was definitely not being good. Perhaps he thought I would not do anything, so he continued whatever he was doing. I whispered to him to stop or I would have to take him out and give him a spanking, and I didn't want to do that. Then I gave him a little hug and smiled. He continued to misbehave, and I picked him up and walked out the back of the church.

A child, even as young as two, can sense when you are uncomfortable, or perhaps feel restrained from disciplining him. If they truly are misbehaving, then I would deal with it.

A grocery store is another prime example of this setting. If my wife really didn't want to use a CLS on our son in a grocery store for fear of getting angry stares or worse, she just took him out of the store. We felt our responsibility to our son came before our desire to get the grocery shopping done and get home at a particular time. We left if we had to, but did not not allow our son to go unchecked.

The earlier parents teach their children to mind

in a public place (and that their disobedience will not be tolerated), the easier it will continue to be. They shouldn't take the route of so many parents who let their children get out of hand because they fear having to discipline or confront their child in a public place.

However, parents need to be aware of how our society, more often than not, is out of kilter when it comes to raising children.

I have a friend who is a doctor, and she had a child brought into her with lots of bruises. The mother said they were from the child's father, but she would never admit that to anyone but her doctor. The doctor called social services and reported this, as she is required to do. They asked her how severe the bruises were, and whether they would be obvious in an hour or two. She said they were not really severe and most of them would not be recognizable in a few hours, and the mother would not be cooperative. Social services chose not to come examine the child even though this was not the first time for this child. Perhaps there are legal reasons why social services could not do anything in this case, but what followed really bothers me.

Several days later, in the same doctor's office waiting room, a mother was having trouble making her five-year-old daughter mind. She took her by the arm and gave her a swat on her bottom, which immediately settled her down. The doctor happened to be walking by, noticed the incident, and thought nothing of it. Someone else in the waiting room called social services, and within fifteen minutes, they were there and took the child from her mother for a short time.

That is not only wrong, it is horrible; but it is

something parents certainly have to be aware of. Perhaps our laws are out of whack. Perhaps in the first case, nothing was done because there were no witnesses to the child's bruises; and in the second case, if a person reports a child being abused, perhaps the law requires immediate action. I am sorry, but when logic and common sense get turned off, we as a society are really headed in the wrong direction.

A TLT or a CLS administered correctly by a calm and reasonable parent, and followed with an overwhelming amount of love and reassurance, is more often than not the correct and most effective thing to do.

But I had a friend who never had to use a CLS after his children got out of diapers because they were so impressionable at that young age. When they were wearing a diaper and did something wrong he swatted the thick diaper with an open hand. It made a loud noise and didn't hurt at all but it sure got their attention and perhaps even scared them a little. Accompanied with a stern voice it made such a lasting impression that once they were out of diapers he only had to use the stern voice and got the same effect. He never had to use a CLS again.

His story reminded me that after my boys turned two or three, I too could get them to mind in most cases with just my stern voice. Children under the age of three are extremely impressionable and the lessons learned there are most likely to be remembered throughout their childhood.

Having said all the above, I must add that no one knows their child better than a parent, and no one is better able to decide the times when a TLT or CLS is appropriate. But as the following story illustrates, there are circumstances when a parent's decision not to discipline a child may be the best choice of all.

First School Picture

Written by Jeanne

I have so many wonderful memories of raising my daughter, but this is one of my favorites, and one of hers too. Kim was in kindergarten at the time and loved it. She was an extremely bright little girl—read by the age of two, potty trained herself before she was fifteen months old, and walked at barely nine months old. She was unbelievably outgoing and precocious.

She couldn't wait to get to school each morning. There were so many new things to learn, and so much fun stuff to do. Her first school picture was due to be taken soon, so we decided to visit my sister, Lonnie, over the weekend and go on a shopping spree for a new outfit. We had a lot of fun that day, but the best was yet to come. My sister gave Kim a beautiful little vanity table, complete with a mirror, chair, and lots of ruffles. Needless to say, Kim could not wait to get it home and start playing with it.

She spent all evening playing at that vanity table, which was now well stocked with combs, brushes, clips, and rubber bands. Every one of her dolls and stuffed animals was given the complete beauty treatment. She was in seventh heaven.

When I awoke the next morning, everything was extremely quiet. Believe me, that was not normal, and I knew in the pit of my stomach something was up. Usually I would simply call Kim to find out where she was and what was happening, but for some reason I didn't. I made my way to her room and silently stood in the doorway. After my initial shock passed, I knew I was looking at a truly precious sight.

She was sitting at the vanity table, smiling into the mirror as she tilted her head one way, then another. Down on the table to her side was a small pair of scissors and a big pile of hair. She had cut off her bangs almost down to the roots, and thought she looked beautiful. To this day, I do not know why my first reaction was not to be extremely upset, but I wasn't—quite the contrary. As quietly as I could, I backed up and went to get my camera. I knew I just had to get this on film. Fortunately, she was so engrossed in that mirror that she didn't hear me come back, so I was able to get the picture I wanted.

When she saw the flash, she turned to me with the biggest smile on her face and said, "Mommy, look how pretty my hair is." She was so proud of herself, felt so grownup, and so pretty; how could I be mad (even with her first school pictures coming up right around the corner)? I told her how pretty I thought she was, and that since she was such a big girl now, that next time I'd take her to the beauty parlor for a haircut.

Well, she had that first school picture taken with her "beautiful hair," much to the consternation of some family members who thought the picture would be ruined. But just the opposite was true. Kim thought it was beautiful, and so did I. It still is one of our favorite pictures. The memories it evokes are sweet and precious.

Besides all the obvious joy of those moments, that incident brought home so clearly to me just how precious our children are. I thank God every day for letting me enjoy that priceless moment. A lot of parents might have gotten angry, and would have missed so much.

Temper Tantrums

With my first four sons, we never had a temper problem. Even Tim, with his aggressive personality, never had temper tantrums. With my fifth son, Daniel, I experienced temper tantrums for the first time. When he was very young, if he did not get his way, he sometimes just screamed. When he was about a year old, I started to try to ignore these tantrums. I could easily tell it was his temper and he was angry, not hurt, uncomfortable, or anything like that. Letting him scream and then cry himself to sleep was one of the hardest things I ever had to do. Sometimes I would stand outside his door, wait for him to take a breath, and rush inside (when he was not screaming or crying) to pick him up.

I figured I wasn't picking him up when he was screaming, so it was okay. Once I picked him up, the screams became sobs; then I could hold and snuggle him, walk with him, and sing to him to settle him down.

Somewhere between the ages of two and three, when I was sure he could understand, I told him I would not pick him up as long as he was screaming. When he had a CLS coming he would cry when I gave him a swat on his bottom; and the crying would stop when I loved him up afterwards. But if he was crying about not getting his way and I paid no attention to him or put him in his room, once in a while the cry would become a scream. I could easily tell the difference. I would go into his room and talk to him. "Daniel, I love you very much, and I know your feelings are hurt. But as your father, I cannot allow you to scream. You are way too good a boy to be screaming like this."

Oftentimes in the beginning, at this young age, the screaming would cease and become just crying or sobbing; then I picked him up and told him how much I loved him, and how I really never wanted to punish him. I'd often say, "It is my job and responsibility as a father to teach you to be as good as I know you are capable of being."

I did not gain a lot of ground in these early years. I just kept at it and tried not to put up with or allow screaming when I knew for sure he understood what he was doing. When he got a little older, I would go into his room and tell him if he kept screaming, I would spank him and give him something to scream about. I had to do that for just a time or two. Then, when the legitimate cry once again became a scream, I would go back in and say, "If you don't stop screaming now, I will spank you again." At this young age, I never had to do it a second time, but I was very lenient on what might be considered no longer crying. The more lengthy and drawn out the confrontation, the more time I spent with him afterwards. I would hug, snuggle, hold, talk to, and play with him until the confrontation became a distant memory; and he once again felt good about himself and his father.

A lot of work, right? But at this young age, the work

was insignificant compared to the problems I would have had later if I had allowed this temper to go unchecked. In most cases a child will not grow out of an unchecked temper. I have seen many adults who cannot control their temper, perhaps because their parents never taught them to.

Each challenge, each temper tantrum, came further and further apart. By the time Daniel was eight years old, he had not had a tantrum in over a year. It was not easy for either of us, but it was sure worth all the time and effort.

As difficult as the job, battle, or confrontation might seem at the time, it will become much more difficult when a child is older. I truly believe it will be nearly impossible once a child becomes a teenager. Either the parents will get lucky and have the tantrums go away on their own, or they will have a teenager they cannot control. If they try to control him for the first time as a teen, they could drive him away, perhaps forever. A child should not have to go through this because parents are unwilling to do what is required of them when he is young. A young child only wants to be loved, and he will forgive over and over. I did my best, kept at it, and tried to be consistent, but I didn't let him throw tantrums.

Again, I stress that after any discipline or confrontation, I always showered my son with positive praise, lots of physical contact, and love. By doing these things, he felt positive about himself and felt very loved, the times of discipline and confrontation soon became less and less frequent. Even during their peak, the conflict seemed insignificant compared to the love and praise

I showered upon him. He loved and respected me in return, and he learned to control his temper.

During those difficult training times, I knew it was important to choose the times for confrontation. I did not allow a really big tantrum or wrongdoing to go unchallenged, but a lot of tantrums and wrongdoings were borderline. So I occasionally choose to overlook something when I did not have an ample amount of time to see it completely through. If I was on my way out the door, for example, and was not willing to give perhaps fifteen or twenty minutes of my time to take care of the problem in its entirety, I was better off ignoring the problem. I did not confront my son and punish him, without following up with lots of positive love and reinforcement. If I did not have the time to see it through to the end, including doubling or quadrupling all the confrontation time with positive reinforcement and love time, then I walked away and faced the issue at another time.

I felt it was much better to be a little inconsistent and overlook something rather than skipping the positive reinforcement. If I had found myself walking away because of this too often, I just rearranged some things in my life, and got my priorities straight.

If a child has a specific problem, such as temper tantrums, then a parent will have to give a lot more of their time to correct the problem. They should be as consistent as possible but they need to make sure they have enough time for any confrontation they choose to pursue.

If they take the time when their child is young, both they and their child will be rewarded for a lifetime.

The Speed Boat

The sharp turn whipped the inner tube around so that it was parallel with the boat, and the boys still hung on.

I continued the circle, creating an ever larger wake. Then I pulled away from the turbulence, turned once again, and headed straight back for it. Just before reaching the raging wave, I cut sharply off to the side, thus whipping the tube towards the wave at twice the speed. When the tube hit the wave, the tube shot over eight feet in the air, and the boys were sent flying. Daniel came down face first as he hit the water.

He popped right back up and seemed okay, but I was really mad at my own foolishness.

I could see he was upset. Angry even. He had a right to be. I could have hurt him.

He swam back to the boat and had trouble getting the bungee cord off the ladder. When I tried to help, he just ripped it off and let it sink into the lake.

I said I was sorry, and he just glared at me.

I really made an effort to let him know how foolish I had been, and how sorry I was; but he just kept to himself or stayed with his nephew the rest of the time we were on the lake.

That night, after I said prayers with him and tucked him in, he gave me a special hug, and said he was sorry for having lost the bungee cord. I couldn't believe it. I, the adult and father, had been foolish and gotten too rough, yet he was sorry for having gotten angry and losing the cord.

I hugged him and hugged him, and told him how sorry I was for being so rough; and how lucky I was to have such an incredible son. Later that night, upon reflection, I thought to myself, "Wow, how unbelievable, and this was a boy who used to throw temper tantrums."

Writing this now, many years later, brings tears to my eyes. How could I be so blessed?

Daniel in Dad's boots

Matt

Special Two

We have all heard it called the Terrible Twos. It is not terrible. It is a very special time.

What makes it perhaps seem terrible is that most children at this age understand much more than we give them credit for, and they are frustrated by their inability to communicate their wants and desires.

We tried to help ourselves and our son by reminding ourselves that he truly understands way more than we could possibly believe. Then we tried to help him communicate whatever he was trying to convey. Some parents even teach their very young child sign language.

Around this age, a child also begins to see himself as a separate identity from his mother and father. He will begin to want to do things his way even more. He will challenge you just to see if he can get his way.

It is natural. We all did it. We taught our son, at this very young age, that he must submit his will to our authority. We did not try to force him to do something if we truly could not see to it that he did it. I was successful with my fifth son, Daniel, in establishing very early that he must take one bite of everything; then if he did not like it, he didn't have to eat it. I established this with praise and positive reinforcement, not with threats. I do not believe you can force a child to eat or take a bite of something.

I did force all my children to come to the dinner table when dinner was being served, even if they were not hungry. I told them that if they did not want to eat, they did not have to, but they had to sit at the table until everyone else was finished. Almost without fail, the sounds and smells of everyone else eating caused them to start eating before the rest of us had finished.

We tried to understand what it must be like to be two. For one thing, a two-year-old finds it difficult to sit still, and so I never really pushed this issue. However, I did not allow my young children to scream or do obnoxious things in church, or leave the table at a restaurant. But I did not try to force them to sit absolutely still.

They tried to emulate me; and if they made a good effort, I ignored all the little squirming around. I tried to never, ever scold or look angry at them in such a setting.

So many parents in a situation such as church or a restaurant will glare or look with anger at their child to try to get them to settle down.

I talked to them beforehand, and I tried each and every time I looked at them to smile and give them a positive feeling towards themselves and the situation. They could not sit still, and I accepted that fact.

Another thing contributing to this Terrible Twos myth is sweets. If we had given our son candy, pop, and other treats, these things would have had an effect, and it would have not been positive. Children will have sugar highs followed by sugar lows, and they won't know how to control those moods.

The amount of sugar many people allow their children to eat is horrible! Sugar is not only bad for their teeth and their bodies, but for their emotional development as well. I have known parents who give their child so much sugar that the child acts hyper, and then they put their child on drugs to counteract the hyperactivity.

All that energy, which even a child not pumped up by sweets has, is normal and good. Parents just need to let them or help them vent it. They can't vent it in front of a TV or by having some miraculous toy entertain them. They need to run and run and play and play. They need to burn off all that energy. Parents should not discourage such activity, but rather should encourage it and should provide them with opportunities to do it. If a two-year-old had to walk behind a parent all day gathering wood or picking berries, he would burn off plenty of energy; and would not seem hyperactive at all. Put the same child in a small apartment with little room to run around, put him in front of a TV, give him pop and cookies, and he certainly will seem about to explode.

Provide a two-year-old with the opportunity to burn off lots of energy. Don't give him sweets and try to understand what he's trying to communicate. Shower him with love, attention, and cuddling. Talk to him as much as possible and more importantly, be with him; then the Terrible Twos will be just another stage of wonder—not only for him, but for his parents as well.

Driving at Two

The summer before Daniel turned three, we were out feeding pairs (cows and calves).

To feed them on my own, I would put the four-wheel-drive into low range, super low gear. Then I would get out and jump in the back as the truck slowly inched its way across the flats.

When Daniel was almost three, he started kneeling behind the steering wheel, pretending he was driving.

At first he did what all little kids behind the wheel do—he turned the wheel back and forth.

Since that made it difficult for me to maintain my balance standing on the back of the truck, I had to teach him that was not the way to drive.

With much praise and encouragement, he soon learned to keep the truck going in a straight line, and was very proud of himself.

After I shoveled the cake (small cubes of high protein cattle feed) off the truck, I would walk up to the driver's side window, thank Daniel for doing such a good job of driving, and ask him to move over.

Then I would turn the truck around and slowly drive by the herd of cows and calves, now strung out across the field, and count them.

One morning, when I got to the driver's side window and asked him to move over, he said, "You get in on the other side."

I did.

He wasn't even three years old, yet he turned the truck around and kept it in a straight line just beside the strung-out herd.

He pretended to count, because he still had not learned to do that yet, but what the heck, he was driving before he was three.

Postscript

I've told this story to others many times in front of Daniel, always mentioning what a big help he was to me; and how proud I was of my son driving before he was three.

Chalk one up for self-esteem.

Mark at age two

What Kind of Toys

Without speaking of safety issues, I do believe parents need to consider what kind of toys their children play with. They should consider choosing toys that are educational and teach motor skills. More importantly, they should be careful of having too many toys that do it all. If all children's toys have bells and whistles and do phenomenal things, they get used to being entertained in this way. They often become bored when they are not being entertained.

A child should learn to use his imagination rather than having his toys do everything for him. Just plain old building blocks are some of the best toys a child can have, or perhaps a big cardboard box he can play in and imagine as whatever he so chooses. Any toy a parent builds for him or he helps build will really be special.

One of the things I truly did not like hearing from my sons or any child is "I am bored." That statement, and a child actually feeling as though he is bored, is partly a result of television, computers, and toys that do seemingly miraculous things.

A young friend of mine told me some people even hand their toddlers iPads. He said, "These kids just sit there with glazed-over eyes, a constant flow of lights and sounds algorithmically designed to enrapture the mind of a child being beamed directly into them through an eight-inch tablet screen." I didn't have any idea that this went on, and I think it is horrible.

Parents need to teach their children the wonder of just being alive, the wonder of a pile of leaves or long grass, the wonder of the clouds in the sky, or the wonder of his imagination. In the past, before all our technology, most children discovered these wonders on their own. Today, we sometimes surround children with so many things that entertain them that they hardly have the time to discover these wonders on their own. A child shouldn't be deprived of learning these things by continually being surrounded with modern technology.

Snake Eyes

Written by Matt

"You've got to be kidding me," I thought to myself as I witnessed the third car in a row weighing in at 4.9-something ounces. I was standing in line with Duggan clutching our carved speedster, dubbed "Snake Eyes." (The name was not based on some significant meaning; a Snake Eyes sticker was the only name included in the decal package we had selected from the local Hobby Lobby.) We had spent several hours cutting, drilling, carving, sanding and painting to achieve our aerodynamic marvel.

I'd like to say we began with a detailed plan of how the car was to look and carefully executed the plan with the precision of a fine furniture maker. The reality was we just went with the flow. We mostly let the wood do the talking. Let its inner personality come out. Yea, that's it.

"Duggan, that's just the way we wanted it." I must have

said a half dozen times as the wood chips fell. It actually came out looking okay. I knew the heavier, the better. (At least that's what the speed kit I purchased along with the decal package said.) Weight equals speed. I was forced to purchase my speed kit as we suburbanites do not possess any spare 22-caliber bullets lying around to double as poundage on our pinewood pace car. (I seem to recall the old man questioning the political correctness of attaching bullets to a nine-year-old's speeding toy way back in the seventies. I can only imagine the pandemonium it would create having live ammunition protruding from the side of a derby car today.)

Now, in addition to a flat chunk of lead to be attached to the underbelly of the car, the speed kit included two types of sandpaper, a white powdery abrasive, four axles (or nails), and a tube of Hob-E-Lube lubricant. I followed the directions for the "fastest car" to a tee, including close to an hour of polishing the axle nails. We attached the nails to a drill, clamped the drill in a vise and ran each through three steps till they shone like "mirrors." (That's what the directions said.) Now at first, I had convinced myself that I was the only dad spending hours sanding nails, so our hard work was sure to pay off. That dream quickly came crashing down as I stood in line at the weigh-in. Everyone, it seemed, had the little bottle of Hob-E-Lube protruding from their back pocket and cars at near maximum weight. Five ounces was the most weight allowed. The rules stipulated once you were at check-in you could take weight off, but not add weight if under the five ounces. My piece of lead had grooves cut through it so we could easily remove a piece or two to lighten up.

"4.5 ounces," the official announced as Snake Eyes straddled the scale. I never dreamt we would be under! I had attached the entire piece included with the kit! All the axle work and we were a full half-ounce lighter than the rest. UUGG!

"Psssst, hey Dad, 4½ is almost 5," Duggan whispered to me almost apologetically. I looked at him and paused, then smiled and ruffled his top.

"You're right, bro, we still have a fast car," I said. Leave it to a kid to keep things in perspective.

The lever dropped at the top of the track. Two cars roll, slowly at first, then picking up speed whoosh their way to the finish where a pillow poufs them to a halt, but not before they pass under a little electronic gate. A light indicator flashes to indicate the swifter of the two. A round-robin format determines the winner in each pack. Eight Cub Scouts in Duggan's pack. Four races for each car, two points to the winner, one to the loser. Top two points leaders advance. Race off in case of a tie.

I'm watching in amazement as Snake Eyes is winning each time! After the last race, I look up at the board and after a bit of quick math, I realize Duggan is the only one with 8 points! He wins his pack! After racing, the cars are quarantined to prevent any tweaks. (Or adding weight.) The next round is against Webelos. Older kids. Heck, I figure the dads aren't any older, so how much better-built can the cars be? Kathleen informs me that our first opponent's car was built with the help of Grandpa.

Grandpa, it seems, is a retired engineer from Lockheed Martin. Gramps and Webelo, it turns out, have spent the better part of the last three weekends perfecting their racer. Needless to say, we are soundly defeated. Second race was much closer, though we lost again to someone else. Never did find out what type of engineering degree beat us that time.

"Just wait till next year!" I tell Duggan later as we are leaving. Already I'm plotting and wondering if there is such a thing as a "Super" Speed Kit.

Interacting with Other Children

A child needs to learn the world does not revolve around him.

He should learn to share, and to get along with other children.

He should learn he cannot always have the toy he wants, and cannot always win at whatever game he may play.

If he has brothers and sisters, this starts at home at a very early age. If he has no siblings at home, parents should be much more aware of the need for this training. Either way, a parent should realize every baby feels the world revolves around him, and he must be taught otherwise..

For this writing, I will speak of getting along with brothers, because this is how my boys first learned about interacting with other kids. The rules and principles are basically the same, even if a child does not have a brother or a sister. It will just be more difficult.

When a new baby brother or sister comes home, the first child will learn he is no longer the sole center of attention. This can be very hard and dramatic for him.

We introduced our first son, Luke, to his new brother or sister in mom's tummy. We talked often with him about the baby mommy was carrying inside of her. We told Luke how much help he was going to be with the new arrival and how important his help would be. Even though my oldest son was only a little over a year old, we still took the time to do these things — not truly knowing how much he understood.

When the new baby arrived, we constantly watched to make sure our oldest didn't feel neglected. We had to give a lot of extra love and time to our firstborn and we made him feel important, because he was the oldest.

When number three came along, the job became much more demanding. Our middle boy, Tim, now had an older brother and a baby brother as well. Shortly after Matt was born, we noticed Tim was becoming quiet, not so full of life. He started going off by himself, which wasn't like him at all. He usually loved running over his older brother's toys and causing all kinds of havoc.

His mother and I had set aside Wednesday nights as our talk night. We had both noticed the difference in Tim and tried to decide what to do about it.

The baby automatically had his place because he was the youngest and Luke had his place as the oldest. The youngest and oldest child have their particular places, but the middle child can feel like he is lost and without a significant position. We decided we needed to devote a lot of extra time and attention to our middle boy, Tim.

We started setting aside extra time for him. Mom was very busy with the baby, so mostly, this was left to me. She did make sure she gave him an extra big hug each night, and she let Tim hold the baby more often. That wasn't so hard, not only because he always seemed to want to do it, but since he had to sit on the couch and couldn't move, he never wanted to do it for very long.

Dad, on the other hand, had to be reminded to spend more time with him. Mom did a good job of reminding me. I was not upset, but rather grateful for the reminder.

One of Tim's favorite things to do was "flying through the air." I lay on my back on the floor and put him on the bottoms of my feet. Then I bent my knees and thrust my feet towards the ceiling. If I did it hard enough, I could send him several feet in the air. Then I would catch him in my hands on the way down. Luke loved watching and seemed to get more excitement out of seeing his brother flying through the air than from doing it himself.

Within a few days of our talk and of taking extra time for Tim, we started noticing he was becoming his old self again. Throughout the years, we had to keep reminding ourselves to look out for things like this.

There were only fifteen months between each one of my older three boys, but there was three years between my third and fourth sons. The principles are the same regardless of the age differences.

We taught our sons to share and respect others. They learned they could not take things away from others, or hit, or push, just because they were angry or had been hit or pushed themself. We were very patient in the beginning.

We, as human beings, must be taught to share. It is not our nature as young children to do so. This required some close observation on our part. Our son soon figured out if we were there, he must share; but he may not have to share when we weren't around. We paid attention and watched when he didn't realize we were watching. We made sure he was sharing and praised him profusely for sharing. We let him know how proud we were of him. At first, he cried and carried on about having to share his things. Most children go through that stage. We allowed him to get used to the idea, but we also enforced his sharing. When two of my boys couldn't share something, I took it away from both of them. In that way, they learned to share more quickly.

Another method I used was to punish both children if either child came to me crying. With my four older boys, it worked very well. If one boy came to me crying about something his brother had done, I would tell him and his brother they needed to work it out, or I would punish both of them. I made an exception to this if a boy said his brother had hit him. If it was obvious he'd been hit (or perhaps the other boy admitted it), then the boy doing the hitting was punished accordingly. Too many times it was, "He hit me first." In that case, I told both boys to work it out, or asked if they would rather I just punished both of them. Funny, they always decided to work it out.

This was a very difficult area to handle, because I would not allow them to come to me every minute complaining about their brothers. I wanted them to know if they came to me tattling on their brother, it better be a pretty serious offense. Otherwise I would just punish them both. In most cases, they learned to work it out among themselves. It quickly got to the point where they no longer came to me about being teased, picked on, or even pushed, because they knew they all would be in trouble. They worked it out among themselves. Once that habit was established, when one of them did come to me, I knew it was likely for a good reason. Parents cannot possibly monitor everything between their children. They should be taught they can't come to parents for everything, even though they feel the other child is doing something wrong.

Something else we considered is that children also tend to be crabby and have more difficulty getting along when they are hungry or tired. My boys would play fine together all day until just before meal times; then they had to be monitored more closely. After supper, and the closer it got to bedtime, the more difficult it was for them. Little things that ordinarily would not be considered the slightest problem now became major problems. We learned to be more tolerant and forgiving of our young sons when they were tired. We monitored them more closely at this time, especially when they were playing with a child from another family. We tried to make sure that play ceased when one or the other got tired.

Of course, there were times when it was impossible to separate our son from a friend when one or the other was tired. Some of those situations can be prevented by making prior arrangements, so when the children get tired, it is time for a child to come home or his friend to go home. Let it be noted, a lot of problems even with children in middle school and high school can be prevented by making sure that they get enough sleep. Too often, our children are cranky and rebellious because they just didn't get enough sleep.

A child should feel good about himself, and think of himself as a good kid. If he is put in situations he has difficulty handling, perhaps because he is tired or not feeling well, then he will need to be continually corrected, and perhaps may come away feeling as though he is not a good kid. The more training, teaching, or correcting a child is given the more positive reinforcement he will need. Yes—this is very time-consuming; but he must come away feeling good and positive about himself.

In the beginning, these intense training periods will be time-consuming, but they will be of short duration. Once a child has learned what is expected of him, it will get easier each day; and only occasional punishments will be required.

When Daniel was young, he interacted very well with other children. When he got a little older, he needed to learn how to deal with his natural gifts and the gift of pride I had helped give him.

Daniel was a born leader and when he was young, he was physically equal or superior to a lot of his classmates. I could see he needed some direction here. He often told his friends what to do; and most of the time, when he competed with them, he won. He took a lot of pride in winning, and couldn't wait to tell me he'd won. This was beginning to be a problem. I talked to him several times about this, but was not able to get through to him. After all, I had taught him to be proud and have a lot of self-esteem; but now I had to teach him how to handle it.

Right after the school year ended and he had completed kindergarten, my six-year-old grandson Brent came to stay with us for three weeks. At first, the two boys really played very well together, and it was great fun for both of them. However, after several days, Brent began to feel uncomfortable; because no matter what they did, Daniel always seemed to win. And to make matters worse, he was very excited about his win. I tried to talk to Daniel again, but still could not seem to get through to him.

Then one day my neighbor dropped off her six-year-old son, Tom. She was unable to pick him up before the three boys went to bed, so I had all three boys all day, that evening, and half the next day. Once again, all three played very well together, but as the day wore on, both Brent and Tom were tired of Daniel always beating them at whatever they did. Instead of trying to talk to my son again, I decided I would try a story. That evening, before they went to bed, I sat down and wrote a story about allowing others to be strong. I read it to them at bedtime.

All the talking I had tried to do before hadn't accomplished what this one story did. The next day, for the first time, I saw Daniel letting Brent win, and actually feeling good about how excited Brent was. When Daniel did win, he praised Brent for how well he had done, rather than bragging about his own win. What I was unable to get through to Daniel in our many talks was accomplished very easily in just one story.

When I went to Daniel's parent/teacher conferences,

I was told what a good teacher Daniel was when he was working with the kindergarten kids. He always seemed to be praising them and encouraging them. He still liked winning when he competed with his own classmates, but when he competed with the younger children, he often let them win.

Allowing Others to Be Strong

*It is a story about two Native American boys who were better than everyone else, but one of them, Little Bear, did not learn his lesson about humility and cooperation, so the other boy later became chief. The complete story can be found in my book, **Stories For All Ages**, which contains several of the stories I used to tell my boys.*

Postscript

When Daniel got older, he was playing cards with his mom, winning all the time and bragging about it. Although she told him that was not fun for her, he continued doing it. When he did it yet again, she said "Okay, Little Bear." His eyes lit up, and he immediately stopped—showing once again the power of a story.

Dad, Mark, Matt and Tim

Story Time

As adults, my older sons have often told me one of their earliest and fondest memories was of story time. I tried to tell my boys a bedtime story several nights a week. I made up stories with morals and lessons in them, using familiar themes like Adam and Eve or some life experience of mine, or just winged it. I realize some people may find this hard to do. If a parent is not comfortable making up stories, then simply get a good storybook. Reading to children at night is soothing and memorable, but occasionally try to make up something or tell a personal story to provide that extra special memory of a story told by Mom or Dad.

Children are especially interested in stories about their parents when they were little, or stories about themselves, grandma and grandpa, or someone else they know. They also like hearing something familiar. I was quite surprised my sons wanted me to tell them a story over and over, night after night. Children even like hearing a story, or a recap if you will, about something they are very familiar with or something that has just happened, like the "Heifers and Root Beer" story following this chapter. We all experienced this adventure, or misadventure, together. They can relive a special moment through the retelling, and by telling it often, they create a story or memory to pass on to their children.

I suggest the non-primary caregiver do most of the storytelling. As the parent who spends the least time with their child, this gives them the opportunity to have close interaction with their child.

I wrote down some of the stories I told my boys in a book, *Stories For All Ages*. Each story contains a lesson, moral, or value. It is okay to tell "Goldilocks and the Three Bears" or similar stories, but it is so much better to tell a story that teaches lessons or values.

In retrospect, I wish I would have told more stories about our country and how it was founded, stories that reaffirm how lucky we are to be Americans and how grateful we should be.

I built a bond with my sons, story by story. A story can also instill values without them even realizing it. Five or ten minutes a night is so little time to give, and such a special time for a child.

Heifers and Root Beer

When my older four boys were about 6, 10, 11 and 12, a bunch of our heifers got loose in the neighbor's woods.

We had just spent the morning and most of the afternoon at the church's annual chicken cookout. These cookouts were put on by the men of the parish, and to keep cool while barbecuing chicken over hot coals, we drank lots of beer.

When we got home and got the news about the heifers, I was a little tipsy, and knew I would really need the boys' help. I told them if they helped me get the heifers back in, they could have root beer floats for supper—all they wanted!

It was very fortunate they came along, because the neighbor fell off his horse several times and was not much help. He had been cooking at the barbeque all day too, and it seems he stayed a lot cooler than I did.

The boys were great and did a great job, but by the time we were done, it was after dark, and like all normal boys, they were hungry again. I never saw anyone drink as much root beer and eat as much ice cream as those boys did that night. They loved it, and were having a ball slurping down root beer, laughing about the neighbor, and talking about the whole incident.

Their mother just rolled her eyes and shook her head. She wasn't so calm the next morning when each one of them woke up sick.

Have you ever heard, "I told you so!"?

As usual, mom was right, but we guys have to be a little bad once in a while, and it did give us a great story that we still talk about today.

All Those Questions

As a child develops, he will ask many questions, and sometimes it seems as though the questions are endless. Often they are questions like "If a dinosaur and a lion had a fight, which one would win?"—a seemingly ridiculous, perhaps even annoying, question.

Don't let it be! A child is learning to sort things out, and he is learning to reason. My number four son, Mark, was so full of questions I felt as if they would never stop. While it was sometimes hard, I tried to smile and understand that to him, these things were important. I just answered, answered, and answered some more. When I got impatient and wished he would just go away, I reminded myself this was an important part of his intellectual development and sense of worth. I could not brush him off. I needed to keep reminding myself he was acting normally; and that my responsibility was to help him feel good about himself and to learn.

If I had cut him off then, he could have cut me off later.

These seemingly unending questions are part of beginning communication between a parent and their child. A child, at this early stage of his development, cannot sit down and have an adult conversation with a parent. Through these questions, he is learning to share thoughts and ideas, and he is learning from a parent—the person or persons most central to his life.

Children give us unlimited love regardless of how many mistakes parents make or what type of individual they are. That love is there in the beginning, and all parents have to do is make sure they do not destroy it. Remember, a parent does not have to earn a child's love—they already have it. They just must keep it.

Realize the power parents have if they use it to teach their son to be all he is capable of being. It can also cement a bond for a lifetime. Parents should answer questions over, and over, and over, then answer more. If they can do this, then their son will keep coming to them when his questions truly have meaning for leading a responsible and full life.

Porky and the Questions

Right after we finished our log home and moved upstairs, we bought a twenty-pound pig.

"Hey Dad, can we name him Porky?"

"Sure." (That was easy.)

"Hey Dad, can he run loose and sleep on the porch like a dog?"

"Hmmm. Why not? Sure." (Not quite as easy, but oh well.)

When Porky got to around one hundred pounds, the boys started riding him around.

By the time he weighed over two hundred pounds, all three boys could ride him at once, and Porky didn't seem to mind a bit.

"Hey Dad, do they make a pig saddle?"

"I don't think so."

When it came time to butcher him, mom and dad were a little concerned about the boys' reaction, so we did it very discreetly (or so we thought).

When we first put the pork chops on the table, we were very apprehensive.

"Hey Dad, is this Porky?"

"Hmmm." (Cough) "Hmm. Yes." (Pause, nervous silence)

"He sure tastes good," one of the boys replied.

Sometime later, "Hey Dad, when are we going to get another pig? Can we get two this time?"

"Okay, why not?"

We did get two, and boy, were they different! We had to put rings in their noses to keep them from rutting up the yard, and they sure loved the mud. As they got bigger, they got mean, and there was no way the boys could ride them.

Then one Sunday morning, we returned from church to find the two pigs in the house on the living room carpet. Of course, they had rolled in the mud first.

The boys and I thought it was funny, BUT NOT MOM!

That was the end of free-running pigs.

A short time after they had been put on the table, it was, "Hey Dad, why can't we get another pig?"

I think I would rather have, "Hey Dad, which is stronger, a dinosaur or a lion?"

Our Most
Valued Gift

Our most valued gift is our time. Nothing a parent could give a child, beyond love, food, clothing, and shelter, is more important to him than a parent's time. A child must have enough nourishing food to grow up to be strong and healthy. He must have clothes to protect him from the elements, a roof over his head, and a place to call home. But do not make the mistake so many people make. A child is much better off with hand-me-down clothes, living in a small home or apartment, and having a parent there, then he is with the finest clothes in a very big expensive home, and not having a parent there. This is not an opinion; this is a fact. Beyond the absolute necessities, nothing—nothing—is more valuable to and for a child than a parent's time.

Just what does giving of our time mean? It most certainly means, if at all possible, having one parent not work out of the home until the child begins preschool. It means one of them being there when he goes to bed. It means having both parents, if possible, being there for the evening meal with him. It means answering all his questions. It means taking the time to see that he does what he is told, rather than more expediently having someone doing it for him. It means giving him as much love, attention, and reassurance as possible after any punishment, to make him feel good about himself while he is learning. It means not using the TV, computer, or other electronic device as a babysitter. It means taking enough time to introduce him to others, and make him feel important. It means going to his school functions, taking the time to look at or help with his schoolwork, and praising him for his efforts. It means parents taking enough time to talk together about his wants and needs. It means realizing that raising a child is a responsibility that requires a lot of time and effort, and then taking on that responsibility.

"There are no ordinary moments," Each of us needs to recognize and remember that as we raise our children. Often we get so wrapped up in our lives and our busy schedules that we forget to notice the beautiful sky, the trees, or the other simple things that surround us. We forget to appreciate how very special each moment with our child can truly be. I do not know if we are capable of always being aware of each ordinary moment, but we should try.

I personally have recently been able to capture many of those otherwise seemingly ordinary moments and have realized how special each one was; but oftentimes in the past I missed out. I hope no one needs to experience what I experienced in order to make them aware of how special each moment is.

I'll share with you a little of what happened, because there but for the grace of God could go each and every one of us. Any of us could be hit by a truck tomorrow; and if we knew we had a very short time left on this earth, we would be much more appreciative of each moment we had. What woke me up to this fact was a medical test. I was truly afraid that my time with my sons might be very limited. Shortly after I received the test results, I had to meet my accountant at 8 am to prepare my income taxes; and you all know how stressful that can be. Daniel had a chapel reading at 9:30 am; and in the past, before my scare, I probably would have thought there was no way I could get there. After realizing I may not have many tomorrow's, I just made sure I got there. He not only read several things in front of the congregation, but he sang several songs with his classmates. When I walked in a little late, I could just see him beam all over. The pride he felt because his father was there was very obvious. As I listened to him read, saw the smile on his face, and the love in his heart, I was moved to tears of thanksgiving for being allowed to share in that moment.

Yes, I had just come from a point where I thought I might not see his eighth birthday, and that truly made me realize how privileged I was to have experienced that moment. But each one of us could be taken today or tomorrow. I was not only rewarded for the special moment I was privileged to share, but I was rewarded again when Daniel got off the bus and gave me a big hug. I was rewarded yet again that night when I put him to bed, and he went out of his way to say, "I love my daddy so much."

I am very relieved to say everything is fine now,

and the fear no longer exists. But it did really make me realize how precious my time with my son was.

I was sad as my sons got older, and I missed those times when they needed me more. I had to resort to doing adventurous things just to keep them interested in doing things with me. Hey! Life should be an adventure.

On the positive side, I didn't have to spend nearly as much time disciplining and guiding as others who had neglected giving their time in those early years. My relationship with my sons became a joy rather than a chore.

As my boys got older still, they had their own agendas—but they were good ones because we had given our time in their formative years.

My wife and I made ourselves take the time for nine or ten years, took joy in those ordinary moments, then relaxed and enjoyed the next eight years. I saw others who convinced themselves they were too busy to give their time during those most important formative years, and they seemed miserable for the next eight years, counting the days until their child left the nest.

Give your child your time. Give him the gift of you.

Spanish Cave: A Family Adventure

When we lived in Colorado, we lived on a remote ranch at 9,200-feet elevation. The highest, most dangerous caves in Colorado were higher than us, and were about five miles away. The entrances to the caves were clear of snow only four to six weeks a year.

I had been to the caves before. In order to get into them, you either had to repel about 150 feet down a rope at one entrance or enter through a much smaller opening that did not require a rope. I figured the older three boys, about 12, 11 and 10 years old, could handle the none rope entrance.

We rode our horses as close as we could, then walked the last grueling mile along a steep mountainside. We all had flashlights and started into the cave on our hands and knees. Soon we were at a spot we could only get through by dragging ourselves on our bellies. When we finally made it, we were not only dirty, but covered in heavy mud.

The cavern was called Marble Cavern and was large enough to hold a small house. As we explored for several hours, I told stories about how the caves got their name from the Spanish conquistadors, who supposedly had hidden gold there.

I told them how some of the old-timers say that at night you could see lights on the mountain by the caves. These were supposed to be lights used by the ghosts of the Spaniards.

All and all, it was a grueling 14-hour day, full of excitement and adventure for my sons. I just didn't realize how much of an effect it had upon them until later.

That night, one of the older two talked in his sleep continuously. The other one kept yelling out something, at least nine or ten times throughout the night. Matt, number three son, walked in his sleep several times, and once even walked right past us and out the front door. Luckily, we were awake to turn him around and head him back to bed.

Values

Truth, Respect, Responsibility, a Good Work Ethic, Self-Esteem, and More

We all have our own sense of values, but the main values I tried to encourage in my sons were truth, respect, responsibility, a good work ethic, and self-esteem. Of these, none is more important than truth. A couple of my bedtime time stories tried to teach this lesson. We knew if our sons were truthful we had it made. But we also knew trying to preach truth would do very little towards instilling it if we did not practice it ourselves. We wanted our sons to be truthful, so we were very careful to be truthful ourselves. We wanted our sons to respect others so we respected them and others. We wanted our sons to be responsible, so we showed them we were responsible. We wanted our sons to have a good work ethic, so we taught them to work. We wanted our sons to have healthy self-esteem, so we praised them over and over to instill self-esteem.

A child will become what he feels his parents think of him; so we let our boys know how proud we were of them and how super each of them were. We kept any criticisms to a minimum and surrounded them with so much positive reinforcement and love that the necessary criticisms were soon forgotten, and only the lessons were remembered.

TRUTH

More than one of my bedtime stories was about truth, and one of them got me in trouble. Before I told them this story, I said something like this, "Boys, I want to tell you a story about Adam and Eve, but I am going to be telling it a little differently than most people tell it, because no one knows for sure how it really happened. This is how I think it could have happened." Then I went on to tell them the Adam and Eve story. Only, in my version, they got kicked out of the Garden of Eden for not telling the truth when asked if they had eaten the fruit. It conveyed the message I wanted to convey. Yet when they were a little older and their Sunday school teacher told the story of Adam and Eve, the boys forgot my caveat and told her she wasn't telling it correctly.

RESPECT

The more we showed respect for each other, family, and others, the more respect our boys seemed to have for us. We also earned their respect by being consistent, so they knew how we were going to respond or act in a particular situation. We actually gained their respect by disciplining or punishing them when they knew they had it coming. They respected us for treating them and their friends with respect. They also respected us for not allowing them to yell at, or talk back to us. A child has no right to yell at or talk back to their parents, and we never did allow this. After my boys reached the age of about seven, they never told me "No"—not once! We earned their respect but we also demanded it.

RESPONSIBILITY AND A GOOD WORK ETHIC

Teaching responsibility begins at a very young age. Children not only have to be taught to pick up their toys, they should be taught it is their responsibility to do it without being told (before they go to bed, for example). This lesson is a very hard thing to teach young children, especially when it pertains to something like picking up their own toys.

Giving them the pride and self-esteem for clearing the table after every noon time meal or feeding the dog is much easier. We told our three-year-old it was his job, then we reminded him of it, and praised him profusely even though at three he was barely able to get it done. Once he knew clearing the table was his job, even though we did most of it, we allowed him to believe he did it—and he was proud of having done such an adult thing. The more adult the responsibility, the more pride a child will take in it, and the more easily he will learn to assume it.

By the time my boys were 7, 6 and 5, they were responsible for doing the barn chores each morning before school. They soon took pride in the fact that they had to work before school and were doing an adult job.

This type of responsibility also teaches a good work ethic, and teaching a good work ethic is easier than teaching responsibility. If our son did his job and did it well, we praised him (even if he had to be continually reminded of the job). We did not take the negative role of correcting or being angry with him for having to be reminded, or for not doing the job as well as he could have. We tried instead to subtly remind him without him realizing it, and then we praised him for having done it without being reminded. We picked out what he did well and praised him for that part, and perhaps added, "And I know you will do better (about some part of the job) next time." We always tried to leave him feeling good about what he did, even if he could have done much better.

SELF-ESTEEM

A good work ethic will come early on, but responsibility may not completely manifest until a child has actually become an adult. Our sons were able to assume some responsibility as they were maturing, and all our direction, teaching, and encouragement ultimately helped them become responsible as adults. We realized that at a young age they may not truly become responsible, but we helped them believe they were. They will become what they believe they are. If a child believes he is truthful, respectful, responsible, and a good worker, he will be these things; and he will have good self-esteem.

Positive reinforcement is a parent's best helper in giving their children values. From my very earliest memories, I can clearly remember my father telling me what a good worker I was. At such a very young age, I know I could not have been a good worker, but that is all I ever heard. My dad even made sure I heard him repeatedly tell others what a good worker I was. I did the same thing with all of my sons, and all of them lived up to what they thought of themselves.

A LITTLE MORE

Let me share something that happened with Daniel when he was between four and five that illustrates the power of truth and positive reinforcement.

When we had a television, Daniel was allowed to watch very little. I allowed one or two hours of cartoons on Saturday morning, but he knew he could not watch Power Rangers or any kind of cartoons that involved lots of fighting or killing. One Saturday morning, when it was really cold outside, Daniel asked if he could stay in and watch cartoons rather than go on the rounds, checking for newborn calves. I said "Okay." When I returned, the television was off, and he told me he had turned it off because the good cartoons were over and only the bad ones were on. I praised him profusely for having done what he was told. I even gave him a big hug and told him how proud I was of him.

The next day, Daniel's friend Tom was visiting. His sister had been on a trip and brought back a stuffed animal for him. He brought it over to show Daniel a few days earlier and had forgotten to take it home with him. When Tom returned, we looked everywhere; but no one could find the stuffed animal. Later I learned that Daniel was very jealous because he did not have one of these himself, so he had hidden it rather than let Tom have it back.

Because I had complimented him so profusely for being such a good boy about watching television, he evidently thought about the stuffed animal, felt badly about what he'd done, and so he "found" it. I asked him where he found it, and he did not want to tell me. He kept saying he didn't remember. I became slightly suspicious then and told him nothing was more important than the truth, and he had to learn to be truthful all the time, regardless of the circumstances. He told me he had found it behind the dresser in his closet. I immediately put two and two together and figured out he had hidden it there. But instead of scolding him for hiding the stuffed animal, I praised him and hugged him for telling me the truth.

I then wrestled in my mind for several hours as to how to handle the whole incident. I decided we needed to have a talk, and I told him it was a very important talk. I was very careful during this talk to tell him how proud I was about his turning off the television. I also praised him for telling the truth about the toy, even though he knew he might be punished if I thought he had hidden the animal.

I proceeded to tell him that we all experience jealousy, and even I sometimes felt jealous about something my neighbor had that I did not. I told him these feelings were normal, but as part of growing up, we had to learn to deal with them. I told him I would not take the neighbor's property and hide it because I didn't have one, and he needed to learn this lesson too. In this round-about way, I made it clear I knew what he may have done. Yet I emphasized he was way too good to have done this, and I was sure he wouldn't do it again. I also reemphasized my praise for his truthfulness.

This was not an easy way to handle this situation. My first reaction was, "How could my son be so thoughtless and cruel?" I wanted to spank him or punish him in some manner, but I did not allow myself to react to my feelings. Instead, I took the time to think and reflect on what would be the best course of action. And positive reinforcement and praise are always the best course of action.

At times a child must be punished, scolded, and reprimanded, but I looked for any opportunity to come at it in a positive way. Children are learning to cope with their natural feelings of suspicion, jealousy, anger, and the like. I tried to guide and teach my sons how to handle these feelings, but I did it in a positive manner. Even though Daniel had done something wrong, the previous positive reinforcement made him want to be as good as I thought he was; and, more importantly, as good as he thought he was. He had learned without being put down, scolded, or punished.

As children are learning, they will make many mistakes. They will perhaps make ten mistakes to every single thing they do right. I tried to gloss over those mistakes, and picked out the one thing they did right, and dwelt on it.

I focused on a positive rather than a negative approach which gave my sons self-esteem. With good values and healthy self-esteem, they could handle anything.

A Grandmother's Wisdom

When I was eleven years old, I was truthful and respected adults. I was still learning responsibility and was just beginning to acquire a good work ethic. But, as with most eleven-year-olds, my self-esteem had a long way to go.

At that age, I loved playing in the sandbox, but somehow I sensed my father did not approve. To this day, I do not know if that really was the case, or if I just thought that was how he felt. He was your typical German. He worked hard, said little, and was very proud.

That Christmas, I remember getting money I was supposed to use to get myself a special gift. I went to the variety store and bought a great cavalry fort set. It had the fort, cannons, lots of soldiers, lots of cavalrymen, and hundreds of Indians. I was really excited about it, but when I brought it home, once again I sensed my father did not approve. I vaguely remember Mom saying she thought I had spent my money foolishly, but this memory, too, may not be correct. I do know I took it back and got something else. The memory that is important is of my grandmother.

My grandmother was visiting when this happened, and I think she knew what was going on. She was aware of my inner struggle. The next day, when I was on the floor playing with some toy soldiers, she came up behind me, put her hand on my shoulder, and said, "Gary, it's okay to play with your toys. You don't have to be ashamed of your wonderful imagination. It is a great gift, and you should be proud of it."

I have always remembered her words.

Thank you, Grandma.

Religion

For those parents who have a deep faith, I need say nothing here because everything they do is based upon their beliefs. Their faith will help both them and their children immensely. I only suggest they teach their children about the love and goodness of their beliefs first. When they teach their children about justice and punishment, I hope they wait until their children have reached the age of reason or older.

For those parents with little or no faith, I suggest that in order for a child to be able to make his own choice later on, he needs to be exposed to some sort of religion or faith early on. The idea of a loving God who cares about and watches over his children is a comforting thing for a child. If a parent is not sure whether this is true, I suggest they still allow their child the benefit of the doubt. For those parents who absolutely believe this is not true, I can only suggest it will do no harm to allow their child to believe it until he gets old enough to make his own decisions. They may be wrong, and as Carl Sagan has said, "Even if there is no god, man would have invented him." Why? Because there is so much benefit derived from living one's life feeling as though you have a purpose, and that someone out there cares and is watching over you. I believe all children should have this comfort.

I have always believed I was blessed with joy and a love of life, but a small gift of faith. Yet those who know me scoff at that. They say the way I live and the way I raised my children shows I do have a deep faith. It is a comforting thought, yet only God knows the truth of it. I think of myself as a good and honest man, but I am certainly not versed in scripture. Yet I have been told by some who know scripture that most of my child-rearing philosophy is absolutely based on scripture. I am not sure if this is true, but I do know this philosophy has been around for many years, and has worked for generations of children. So perhaps some of it is scriptural because prior generations were more religious and deeply faithful.

I will share a couple of things here that I wrote many years ago.

The Gift of Life

The greatest joy is in sharing. And when a gift is given the greatest thanks that can be returned is knowing the gift has brought great joy. The greater the joy, the greater the reward to the giver.

Did not our God want to share, did He not give us the gift of life and is it not safe to assume that the best way to thank Him is to live life and love it?

I put to you that we should not seek to suffer but rather, for our Lord, we should seek to be happy, for it is in our happiness and in our sharing of this happiness with others that we show our greatest love for God.

Is this not why He made us?

God Is

God is. This much I feel, this much I some-how know. Beyond that, I can only hope.

No man can tell me what I must or must not believe. He can only suggest what he believes to be true.

If his truth is truth, and I do not see it, am I guilty of sin?

What is sin?

May I suggest that sin is only what you know it to be? If one has doubts, is it not reasonable to face them and form an assumption rather than to act on instinct, feeling or command?

Each one of us must find our own obligation and fulfill it. And if others seek our help, help. If others try to thrust their duties and obligations upon us, help if you wish; but always forgive and love them.

Only God can damn you.

Only God—if indeed God ever would.

Live your life, fulfill your dreams, and give to God all that you do and all that you are.

For a man can give no more.

TV, Computers, Cell Phones, and More

Each and every one of us are part of all we experience. Everything that touches us has an effect, and children are particularly susceptible to all that they experience. My wife and I tried to control as much as possible the experiences of our sons. We tried to fill their experiences with love, joy, values, and positive things. We also tried to maintain some measure of control. I think that would have been nearly impossible if we had allowed our sons free access to TV, computers, gaming systems, cell phones, or the like.

We raised our first four sons, mostly without a television in our home. About the time our oldest son turned six or seven, we bought our first TV. Computers, video games and cell phones were not readily available back then. We monitored our boys' television time. Each boy chose one hour of TV a week, and they could watch each other's choices. They could also watch mom and dad's hour, so they got to watch about six hours of TV each week. This encouraged them to read more, and spend more time playing and using their imagination. The boys eventually liked to read so much that we actually talked about restricting their reading! We wanted them to experience their own life adventures, rather than just those in a book.

As a single parent, raising my fifth son, Daniel, was more difficult for me. It would have been very easy to put Daniel in front of the TV and use it as a babysitter. The advent of VCRs, DVDs and streaming media made it even more tempting. Yes, screens can be used in a beneficial way. Educational programs can benefit children. These programs can entertain and delight them while teaching. Couple all these positive benefits with the benefit of giving a parent a truly needed break and you can see how parents tend to overuse screens. Even if children are monitored, and are exposed to only beneficial programs, parents should be careful not to overuse these things.

My wife and I wanted our sons to experience life through their own experiences rather than to experience it through the experiences of others. We wanted them to develop their own imaginations and to explore the world around them. We felt they needed to learn to entertain and challenge themselves, rather than always having something entertain them. They needed to discover the wonder of a book or a piece of paper and a color crayon. They needed to be around and watching us, even in our daily mundane tasks. They needed to be interacting with us. And they needed to gain self-confidence to be able to create or make their own experiences.

Even when all the programming a child watches is of a good nature, too much time spent on it can deprive him of other things. To adults, these things may seem insignificant, but they truly are important in a child's development. A child also is learning lifelong habits—if he is put in front of a TV every day, then he will more likely continue this habit throughout his life. Once free access to TV, tablets or computers has been established with a young child, It will be difficult to curtail later on. A child will expect to be able to use the TV, tablets, gaming consoles, cell phone, or computer whenever he wants (See the chapter "What Kind of Toys").

A child will truly be affected by all that he experiences and should not be allowed to see violence over and over. He will become numb to that violence. Watching acts of deception, a good con man, or thief is even worse!

Deception or a clever con may be entertaining in a movie, but it gives a child the wrong message. The message is to see how much you can get away with. The hero is a good thief or a clever con artist. The people being conned are, more often than not, being conned because they are good, trusting people—people portrayed as being nerds, stupid, and not cool.

In the past, children heard stories and tales about their family and heroes. The stories were told by people who cared for and loved them. The stories brought a sense of closeness and taught values or at least gave children the messages parents wanted them to receive. I do not believe movies, TV, video games and the like are telling the right kind of stories or giving the right messages.

If nothing else, having these things strictly monitored will force a parent to spend more time with their child, and time is their most precious gift. Certainly parents can sit down and watch a movie with their child, and have it be a positive sharing experience. More often than not, however, parents tend to put their child in front of a screen and go about their other daily business. A child learns no self-esteem by watching a movie. He learns self-esteem by being in his own movie of life.

PHONES, PEER PRESSURE & SOCIAL MEDIA

I will admit when raising my boys, I didn't have part of the country and social media pushing a lot of the things I disagree with. My boys were proud of being different and not affected by peer pressure. Even as adults, my sons have little to do with social media.

I also talked to a couple of young parents who have raised and are raising their kids while dealing with social media. In both cases they restricted the use of social media in some manner and they went out of their way to find groups and families who shared their values.

Television, computers, cell phones and social media contribute heavily to peer pressure. If a child learns to experience life through a parent, through his own initiative, or that of his siblings, then he will be building self esteem. He will be less susceptible to what society or his peers may be doing or thinking. Television, on the other hand, promotes peer pressure. It promotes doing as others do, and worrying about what others think. Commercials are not just selling their product. They are selling the very idea of peer pressure. The younger the child, the easier it is for parents to turn the TV on to help out. Perhaps they think that at this young age, it can do very little harm. I believe the opposite is true.

The younger the child and the more television he is exposed to, the more profound the effect.

If a child is taught in the early formative years not to need the pacifiers of modern technology, then the more likely he will be able to use it wisely later. Parents can also use these restrictions as a form of teaching their child he must submit to their will.

Wow, this is where a parent's early groundwork had better have been very good. Almost no one else will restrict their child in regards to these things and he will say, "All my friends can do what they want."

When parents feel the time is appropriate for him to have a phone, I suggest it should be one that only allows him to receive and make calls. Now he can reach a parent and a parent can reach him without exposing him to all the other BS.

Once a normal cell phone is allowed I would consider doing as some good friends of mine did. They required their children to drop their cell phones in a basket each night before they went to bed. The kids could take them out of the basket the next morning just before leaving the house. Now the parents could check the phones and and even their computers each night to make sure the kids were not using them in the wrong way.

I don't like social media at all. If it is allowed I suggest it be controlled. I would wait until they were 16 or 17. I would also install parental control software on their and or family computers to restrict access to sites I disapproved of and to enforce time limits.

Until he reaches a certain age I might even consider buying an air-gapped computer, one incapable of getting on the internet. He can learn to type on it and do school assignments, but he won't be able to get on the internet. If he is required to do something on the internet, he can use a school computer at the library or a parent's computer at home.

These so-called smart phones are worse yet. It has been proven they are absolutely addictive. I have seen families in restaurants sitting at a table looking in their lap at their smartphones and not interacting with each other at all. I would keep them out of their lives until they were at least fourteen. If parents have done most things right for fourteen years, their son will be able to handle it then.

At very least no smart phones or other devices should ever be allowed at the table. Not at home, visiting, or out to eat. That means for the parents, too! Communicate and connect with each other and not through some device. This is a rule parents can insist on. It is extremely important and it is just plain good manners.

If a child has healthy self-esteem, and feels part of a strong family, he can be taught to be proud of being different. Then one of the most damaging things to a child's development, peer pressure, will not affect him at all.

What Our Stories Say About Us

Written by Tim

I'll cut a movie some slack if the overall theme is good, a positive or true underlying message or basic premise.

Movies that glorify or make 'cool' the wrong things I don't necessarily always hate—but they start out with several strikes against them.

It's also one of the points I made about Matrix 3—it's one of the horrible ways that Hollywood corrupts, in the most basic and true sense of the world, the character of the nation.

It's why most people don't even consider right and wrong—only what they think they can get away with—because that is the message of most movies and almost all of TV.

There have always been movies and books and stories about the outlaw, the bad guy. But even if the character was sympathetic, usually he either displayed his own moral code or the story ended tragically or both.

Cultures and values throughout history have been propagated and passed to the next generation by a society's stories and myths. Cultural anthropologists analyze a culture's legends and stories to tell them things about that culture. We all have read Aesop's Fables, Grimm's Fairy Tales, American Folktales—they all say things about the cultures that told and enjoyed them. I've always loved stories and fables. Tell me what your favorite stories are and I'll tell you who you are.

What do our movies, stories, and cultural 'myths' say about us? Do they say that we are shallow, greedy, vain, and materialistic opportunists? Like you Dad, I hated—HATED!—that Tom Cruise movie with the catch-phrase "Show me the money!" And it became a huge hit and that disgusting catch phrase became an American pop culture icon.

A people's character is revealed in their stories—America's favorite stories are corrupt—can her people be any different?

Postscript

Tim, I hope so, and the first step in rebuilding the character of a nation is to build the character of the nation's children.

Friends Overnight

Having friends stay overnight or having a child stay overnight with his friends is something parents should give some serious thought and consideration to. Certainly, when friends or relatives are visiting, an overnight stay may be necessary. A parent should decide whether to allow overnight stays to be the norm, only for a special occasion, or perhaps, as in my son's case—almost never allowed. I preferred to drive in and pick my son up at bedtime and bring him back the next morning rather than allow the overnight stay. If the boys were camping or getting back very late from a school event, and it was impossible for me to pick them up, then I made an exception. But I never allowed it just to save myself a late night or early morning drive.

For young children, I do not believe staying overnight causes any problems, other than perhaps a little less sleep. But once allowed, a child will come to expect this, and it will be difficult to stop later on. Perhaps no harm would come of these overnight stays, but the potential risks far outweigh any benefits. A parent has little or no control on overnight excursions. A child is subject to more peer pressure on these overnights.

He will be more attuned to doing what his friend may ask or more apt to be influenced by his friend's action than normal. None of my boys stayed overnight or had others stay over unless they fully understood that it was an exception due to some particular circumstance. They all complained and said that everyone else was doing it. No matter, I stuck to my guns. Perhaps this too was a small lesson in, "It doesn't matter what everyone else is doing. We do it our way."

As a child, I was allowed to go on overnights and have others over. On these overnights, I learned to sneak, I learned dirty jokes, I saw my first nude magazines, I snuck out of the house for the first time, I tasted my first hard liquor, I started talking on the phone for hours, and I was perhaps more influenced by my friends' thoughts and actions than at any other time.

My sons were not affected by peer pressure, and I believe this was a small but contributing factor. Remember, standards are being set. A young child will be disappointed that he cannot take part in overnights, particularly when he knows other young children are doing so, but he will accept it. A teenager will not accept the fact that he can't stay overnight or have others overnight if they have been allowed in the past. It will be difficult enough to deny him the overnight (even though they have never been allowed before), because all his friends will be doing it. He will certainly try to get his parents to allow it now. Parents need to do what they think is best for their child, but they should be aware of the dangers, and not allow it just because others do.

After I wrote the above, I started to allow Daniel to stay overnight and to have friends here overnight. I realized that with my older four sons, the "no overnight rule" was acceptable because they had each other. They were close enough in age to be able to play together and not feel as though they had no one to play with.

Daniel, my fifth son, on the other hand, was like an only child. We also lived on a remote ranch, and he truly had no one to play with. I also took into account that he was a terrific kid who did more than his share of work around here. More importantly, I perceived him as very trustworthy. It was very difficult for him to get together with friends without occasionally allowing him overnight stays. I relented, and did allow it. As I have said, each child is different, and parents must weigh all the facts and options, and then choose what they perceive to be the best course of action.

I still believe I was increasing the risks when I allowed these overnights, but I hoped that because of who Daniel was, the risks were acceptable. I remained very aware of these risks and monitored these overnights as closely as I could. In the end, nothing bad came from any of the overnights.

Overnight

We didn't allow our four older boys to have friends overnight, but we had all kinds of family overnights. We camped out in the boundary waters of northern Minnesota, on the mountains of Colorado, in the back pasture, in the backyard, and on the living room floor.

I'll share one of Mark's memories of a family overnight. When writing this book, I asked Mark if he remembered going into Spanish Caves with his older brothers and me. He said he never went to the caves, but he did remember one time when the whole family camped out on the mountain just below the caves. Here is what he remembered.

All of us rode horseback to a little clearing on a creek, about 1,000 feet below the caves. We were all supposed to go caving, but after the long ride, the climb looked like a little too much for Mom and Mark, who at the time was only six. The older three boys and Dad went up to the caves, and Mark and Mom decided to stay back and do a little relaxing on the mountain.

When we returned from the caves, we cooked our dinner over an open fire, sat around the campfire telling stories, and talking about the day's adventures.

The tent was pitched alongside the creek, and in the middle of the night, someone noticed that Matt was missing. When he didn't answer our calls, we went looking for him. He was on the other side of the creek, walking around in his sleep. He had also walked in his sleep the last time he'd been caving.

Matt managed to make that walk across the creek (in his sleep) without getting wet. When I went over after him and woke him up, he was very drowsy. On the way back to the tent, he managed to fall in the creek. That sure woke him up!

Funny what a six-year-old will remember. Just your average overnight.

Communication

Communication is a necessary lifeline between parents and their children. No matter how unimportant, trivial, or even nonsensical it may seem, parents should give their children their ear.

The younger a child is when the bridge of communication is built, the easier it will be to reinforce and strengthen. Yes, giving so much time with a toddler just learning to speak is not easy, but this time will be well invested. Parents can build the line of communication early on and reap the benefits throughout a child's upbringing.

My wife and I communicated lovingly with each other in front of the children. We took the time to sit down together with our son or sons and have a talk. Another way we encouraged communication among our family was by having a set dinnertime where we were all together. We talked about the day's events and other things, and we tried to keep this mealtime unhurried. No one was allowed to leave the table until everyone was finished. We kept the television and radio off during our evening meal.

Having a radio on all the time may be soothing to some, but it may prevent or discourage the communication which could be developing between a parent and their child. Having the television on in the background or having it be a companion for a child will really hinder communication. When a child is awake and around, I suggest it be left off. If a parent likes having the radio on, I suggest they consider waiting until the kids are asleep or gone. Parents should consider staying off of computers and cell phones as much as possible when the kids are around. Not allowing the kids unlimited time on a computer or a cell phone will also encourage or at least allow communication.

When I was doing a mundane job, I often talked to my son as I worked, even when he was out of hearing range or seemingly too young to understand. No one called the men with the funny white jackets, and my son often did hear. Believe me, when a teenager is experiencing trouble, difficulty, or peer pressure, if he feels as though he can talk to a parent about it, then the parent and he have it made. If parents pay the price early, they can enjoy their son's teenage years while still being able to help and guide him.

Telling bedtime stories was part of the formula I used for developing future communication. More importantly, no matter how silly or foolish my son's questions may have seemed, I treated them with respect, and answered them the best I could (See the chapter "All Those Questions").

Another important part of communication is the communication between parents. My wife and I tried to talk often about how our children were doing. If one of them was having a problem, then both of us would try to concentrate on giving that child extra attention.

If sharing and talking about the children comes easily and naturally for parents, it will benefit their children greatly. On the other hand if it is difficult for one or both parents to take the time out of their busy schedules to discuss the children, then I strongly suggest setting aside one evening a week to talk about the kids. Take that time to discuss problems, feelings, or insights about the children. Mention any developing problems or a particular need that must be addressed for one or all of the children. Then discuss the best way to tackle whatever needs to be accomplished. This discussion time will be of particular benefit when it comes to helping their child relate to other children, and may even have the added benefit of helping parents build overall communication between themselves.

Communication has been kind of easy for me, when I have taken the time to do it, but with my older four boys, I missed a lot. I can remember going to my uncle's cabin when his whole family was there. I remember how much time they spent as a family just sitting by the fire talking. At the time, I just didn't understand it.

I was always trying to get them to play cards or a game, or to go outside and play Starlight/Moonlight, or whatever.

Even as a newlywed, I never enjoyed sitting around visiting. I always wanted to be doing something. I can even remember getting up and dancing, even if there was no music. It took the maturity of age to make me see the light.

One night my thirteen-year-old son, his mom, and I sat in the living room visiting for the first time I could remember. We must have talked for over two hours, and I can't even remember what we said. What I do remember is how good it felt.

The next morning he told his mom how much he had enjoyed talking the night before. Several weeks later, when I asked him what he wanted to do after supper, he said he wanted to sit around and talk. He wanted his parents to share some of our childhood memories, and he shared some of his. I can not tell you how nice it was. I'm only sorry I didn't discover it earlier, so I could have done it more often with more of my boys.

If a child always has easy access to the radio, the TV, the computer, cell phones or the like, then moments like this will probably never happen. Before cell phones, I did not allow my boys to be on the phone too long. We allowed short phone calls and occasionally an hour call, once a day. Now I see kids being on their cell phones all the time. The first thing they do in the morning is get on their phone and then seem to be constantly using their phone throughout the day. NO WAY! I would not allow it.

When my granddaughter was going to come to the ranch for a week, I told her she couldn't bring her cell phone. She said then she wouldn't come. I said, "Okay, then don't come." She came anyway, without her phone. When she left, she said it was so nice not having her phone that when she got home she was going to be on it a lot less. Her father told me she lasted about two weeks and then she was living on her phone again.

WOW! Keeping a child off their cell phone all the time when all the other kids are on theirs will be tough. Parents better establish communication with their young child early before they wind up giving them a cell phone. Not only is cell phone use a real, diagnosable addiction, sadly, now it has been accepted as normal. That is why I would keep cell phones out of their lives as long as possible. Without that distraction, communication will be much easier.

Parents can also communicate with their children in many other ways, including with their loving smile, and their hugs, and kisses.

My oldest son, Luke, tends to be reserved. He once told me he felt awkward when he first started making sure he kissed his wife goodbye every morning, and hugged and kissed his boys at bedtime each night. Now, after many years, it has become a habit he is very comfortable with. He knows kissing his wife each morning strengthens their marriage, and he was pleasantly surprised that even as his boys got older, they still looked forward to his goodnight hug and kiss.

When Luke's youngest brother, Daniel, was 14 years old, he too still looked forward to his hug and kiss each night.

What a beautiful form of communication!

Going Potty

Moms often seem better able to handle sick children than dads. There are a lot of other things that moms seem to handle better than dads—at least this dad.

I tried the best I could to be both mother and father to Daniel when he was young, but the following story illustrates that despite my best efforts, as a mother, I left a lot to be desired.

Before Daniel was born, I did almost everything on the ranch by horseback. Once I had him with me full time, I had to adapt to a pickup or a jeep so I could take him along wherever I went.

Daniel was with me almost constantly. The ranch was over six miles long, and even before he was potty trained, he saw me relieve myself whenever I felt the need.

After he was potty trained, he too relieved himself wherever he found himself on the ranch. By the time he was three, he also had no difficulty squatting and doing number two if the need arose.

When he was playing in the yard, it was too much trouble to come inside, so he just went potty in the yard. We were over two miles from our nearest neighbor and lived in a large valley where you could not see anyone else's lights (let alone another house), so dad, being a dad, said nothing.

It never occurred to me that when he was visiting his mother, who lived in a suburb, he just might potty in her yard.

She never said a thing to me about him peeing in her yard, but I sure heard about it when he decided to pull his pants down and do a number two in her yard.

I guess if he'd had a full-time mom around, he would have been taught more appropriate behavior (Smile!).

Making Mistakes

All parents are going to make many mistakes. They are going to get angry. They will lose their patience. They will not listen. They will forget a promise, and they will be less than they—and their child—knows they should be. Parents should not worry too much about these missteps. They just need to do their best and recognize and learn from them. If they truly do their best, recognize and learn from their mistakes, their child will understand.

Parents should learn from their mistakes when their children are young, and make fewer as the children grow older. I continue to be amazed at how young children forgive and forget. Young children unconditionally love their parents regardless of the kind of people they are.

As my son got a little older, I even talked to him about my mistakes and apologized for them. It was a time I could shower him with love and gratitude for understanding and forgiving me. I continued to build the bonds of respect and love when they were young, and they continued to forgive me even when they got older.

I also made mistakes I did not recognize. When my

boys were perhaps 10 or 11, I told them that if I made a mistake, they could talk to me about it. However, after they talked with me, if I didn't feel as though it was an actual mistake, then they would have to forgive me and live with it. They did!

I made many mistakes, but one stands out. When Daniel was six, he had three other six-year-old friends over one afternoon. They played outside most of the day and were typical boys of that age. When I asked them to help me, they gladly agreed. I was preparing a yard to be planted in grass seed and was raking it smooth. I asked the boys to pick up a few rocks from the yard and throw them in the ditch. They were doing a good job and having a lot of fun doing it. But as time went on, a couple of the boys started to get bored. My son Daniel encouraged them and made it fun again. I was really proud that he wanted to help and encouraged his friends to help.

A lot of the fun was throwing the rocks, and I told them several times to be careful not to hit one another. They didn't seem to hear me, and bounced rocks off one another's arms or legs occasionally. I growled at them, but they didn't seem to heed the warning. First and foremost, I probably should have stopped them from throwing the rocks. In retrospect, it seems obvious that one of them was bound to get hurt, and I should have prevented that. Second, I was not particularly happy with having to do this job. I had arranged for a teenager to do it for me, but he canceled at the last minute.

Sure enough, it finally happened. One of the boys got hit in the head. I made sure he was all right, then asked who did it. Daniel pointed at the other children, and they said Daniel had done it. I lifted him to his feet by his arm and spanked his bottom.

Daniel had been particularly good the past two or three weeks, and I was proud of how he encouraged his friends to help me work. I also had not spanked Daniel in perhaps six or eight months, or even longer; I really should have thought about spanking him in front of his friends. More importantly, I should have not allowed him to be in a position that resulted in someone getting hurt. My emotions also played a part in my actions.

I had made a mistake, and Daniel's continued crying made that obvious. He did not cry for so long out of pain, but rather because his father had done the wrong thing, and had even done it in front of his friends. I went over to him and told him how proud I was of how he was working and encouraging his friends to work. I said I was sorry to have had to spank him, and that I never would have done it if he had told me he had hit his friend. Then I gave him a big long hug, held him in my arms, and said, "I love you so very much." He was still feeling hurt and down so I got up, started helping the other boys pick up rocks, and made a game out of it. I was an airplane dropping rocks in the ditch, bombing other rocks. Daniel got caught up in his friends' excitement over the game and joined in. The crisis was over and hopefully forgotten—forgotten by him, but added to my learning experiences about being a parent.

In proof reading this several years after it was first written, I cannot tell you how that memory still bothers me. How could I make such a mistake, and how could I even be forgiven? When I shared those feelings with my best friend, she said I shouldn't be sad because we all make many mistakes. Some are worse than others. "It is how a parent handles their mistakes that makes them a good parent or a poor parent."

A Long Walk for a Little Boy

A mistake that I didn't know I had made

This is a story I did not hear until several years after it happened. I was sitting around with a couple of my boys reminiscing about old memories when Luke told me this story for the first time.

The boys had to walk about a half mile down the driveway or a quarter mile through the woods to catch the bus and we couldn't see the bus stop from the house. Luke, with his easy-going nature, was a little slow getting out of the door for school each morning. One day, his brothers told me the bus driver had to wait for him, and told Luke the next time he would leave him.

In an effort to emphasize his responsibility, I told him if he ever missed the bus, he might just have to walk to school, because I probably wouldn't take him. I thought this took care of the problem, and that he never missed the bus.

Several years later, I found out he did miss the bus one day—and just started walking to school. We lived out in the country and were seven miles from school. At the time he was only in second grade.

He got two miles down the gravel road when, thankfully, a neighbor stopped to ask him what was going on. The neighbor had him get in and took him to school. No one—not the neighbor, Luke, or his brothers—told me the story until many years later.

Postscript

I would have been very nervous, upset, and angry at myself for making such a thoughtless threat, had I known at the time he would start walking instead of asking for my help. This time turned out okay, and may even have done some good, but the risks were not worth the gain. I tell you the story now, so you will be very careful what threats you make to your child.

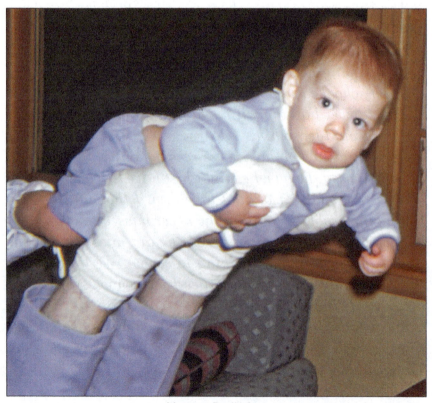

Matt on Dad's feet

Hidden Secret to Healthy Self-Esteem

Perhaps part of the reason Daniel could bounce back so quickly (even when his father made a big mistake in front of his friends) is because he had such healthy self-esteem. So high, in fact, that he could overlook and forgive my mistakes. They were just mistakes made by his father, who he loved very much. Many things contributed to his positive self-esteem, but I have one special secret to help instill healthy self-esteem in a child.

A young child looks at his parents all the time. He is watching even when they don't realize it. He notices their actions and their looks of approval or disapproval. If each time a parent notices his gaze and they give him a loving smile, he will feel good about himself. A smile shows him he is liked. A parent's feelings and their opinions are very important to him. His feelings and opinions, like it or not, are largely formed by his parents' feelings and opinions. If a parent continually shows him he is liked, he will like himself.

Parents should try to teach their son all he needs to know, and they need to correct his mistakes. It is right that they do so. But a young child is going to make mistakes daily, hourly, and sometimes continually. He will be too noisy, he will spill his milk, he will not pick up his toys, he will not share, he will not want to go to bed, he will get dirty, he will come into the house with mud on his feet, he will run with a sharp object, he will pester and whine—the list goes on and on.

Human nature directs parents to try and help him shape up, to constantly tell him how to do better: I told you to be quiet, I told you to pick up the toys, look what you did to my carpet, why are you not ready yet, and here again the list goes on and on. To continue to learn, children will, and must, make mistakes. If parents are continually pointing out those mistakes in a stern or negative way, their son will soon feel negatively about himself. All the mistakes a child makes while he is learning and growing tend to test a parents patience. Parents struggle to keep from being stern or correcting each misstep. It is even more difficult to smile in a loving manner when a parent is nearing the end of their patience, but they need to do just that!

I always tried to find one thing out of ten my son did right, and I praised him for it. When he was feeling good about himself, I casually mentioned that I was sure he would pick up his toys next time (or whatever other lesson I wanted to convey), and I did it with a loving smile.

One morning when Daniel was about five years old, I told him to quickly take a bath before school. He took longer than he should and had a little fun along the way. When I hollered at him to hurry up, the next thing I knew he was standing before me in the living room buck naked. My human nature wanted to say, "Why aren't you dressed? What are you doing here?" but instead, I looked down at him and smiled. He hugged my legs and said, "I love you, Daddy." Then I could say, "Come on now, we have to hurry up." He did hurry to the best of his ability, and he did so feeling good about himself. Why he needed that hug at that time, I do not know. Perhaps he was even feeling guilty or bad for playing a little too long in the tub. Whatever his reason, my smile made him feel good about himself. Moments like this are really important in building his self esteem.

Church is another example of a particular situation where a parent may be tempted to give stern looks. My sons seemed to be continually looking at me during church, and each time I noticed their gaze, I smiled at them. Often they were looking at me because they had just done something—like trying to put the kneeler down, dropping it, and making a loud noise. They looked at me to see if they had done something bad. Most parents, without even thinking, will scowl at their child for having made the noise. In their desire to teach their child reverence and respect, some parents seem to be always scowling or looking sternly at their children. They would accomplish so much more if they instead gave their child a loving smile. The child would feel better about himself, and he would feel loved and comfortable in church.

Perhaps a young child looks at a parent so often in church because he truly has trouble sitting still and is always fidgeting or moving around. He senses he should be better, so he looks at his parents. Yes, their scowl or stern look confirms he should be sitting still, but he can't do that. If his parents continue to look stern and upset with him he will begin to feel bad about himself. He may even begin to feel uncomfortable in church.

When my sons were a little older, they sometimes did something in church they knew they should not have done. I showed them with a stern look that yes, I noticed they had made a mistake, but I immediately followed that with a warm, loving smile.

A parent will sometimes find this a difficult thing to do, especially when they are not feeling well or other things are upsetting them, but they will find it worth every ounce of effort required. When a parent pays attention, they will be amazed by how often their child looks at them to see if they are angry, stern, or smiling. Smile! Smile at him and show him he is loved, and he will love himself.

This is such a simple gift that parents are able to give their son, and it will have a monumental effect. More importantly, the absence of this gift can erode their son's self-esteem.

A child will continually make mistakes as he learns. If parents give in to human nature and look sternly at him, he will look sternly upon himself. Show him he is loved. SMILE!

Smiles A Lot

You might like to read a story I wrote about the power of a smile. The story "Smiles A Lot" can be found in my book, **Stories For All Ages**.

More on Truth

Along with a smile being a valuable tool, truth is an even more valuable one. I taught my sons very early that nothing was more important than truth. One of their favorite bedtime stories was a story about truth, love, and strength. The story taught the lesson that even love could not survive without truth. If parents can establish truth with their children, they truly will have it made.

In order to establish truth as a value, I talked about it often. I told my sons how important I felt it was. I also tried to be truthful all the time myself, and at times, I found it not easy to do. As adults, we feel it is okay to tell a little white lie, especially if it is for the benefit of those we are telling it to, but young children will not understand this gray area. For example, you tell someone on the phone you are working so you can't come over to help, and your child sees you watching a movie instead.

Not only was I careful to be truthful around my sons, but I was careful in disciplining them where truth was involved. If I was not absolutely sure my son was being untruthful, I did not punish him. A child who has, in fact, been truthful will find it very difficult to understand why he is being punished for telling the truth. When I was not sure, I always gave him the benefit of the doubt or avoided the issue. If I felt my very young son was not being truthful, I might check up on him, so I would know with absolute certainty whether he was telling the truth or not. For instance, I would watch him when he didn't realize I was watching. When he did something I felt he may not be willing to admit to, I asked him later if he did this particular thing. If he lied, then I punished him appropriately. In this type of situation, if I spanked his bottom, it was harder than normal, and I explained why. I wanted him to know nothing was more important than truth, and telling a lie was a very serious offense.

Whenever possible, I avoided putting my son in a position where he may have been tempted not to tell the truth. I did not ask him about every little thing. In the beginning, he was just not going to be able to handle telling the truth all the time. So I didn't ask. I didn't put him in a position of being tempted to lie. I tried to find out the truth for myself and didn't put him on the spot unless absolutely necessary or I already knew the answer.

When he was learning to be truthful, and did something wrong and was truthful about it, I overlooked the wrongdoing. I praised him instead for having told the truth, even though he feared he might be punished. I cannot emphasize enough the importance of establishing with a child the fact that he can be trusted to be truthful. I believe it would be impossible to establish that kind of rapport if a parent continually put him on the spot. They should not tempt him to lie. When a very young child spills his drink, he will know and sense he has made a mistake. If he is asked "Did you spill your drink?" he may say "No" out of self-defense.

When he is learning, don't ask. Don't tempt him to tell an untruth. Help him to be truthful. Ask him questions he can easily answer truthfully.Then praise him for his truthfulness.

When my sons were teenagers, I talked to them about my teenage years. I told them I was always truthful, but I wasn't perfect. I was able to be a little wild, and yet still be truthful, because my father gave me a little leeway. This talk seemed to bring them closer to me and increased our bond. Even if a parent was perfect as a teenager, they are going to have difficulty getting their child to believe that. Parents should let their hair down a little with an older son, and that truthfulness will bring him closer to them.

Parents have all heard how important it is to always know where their child is and who he is with. I agree, but with this caveat. If he is not in a bad place or situation, consider allowing him a little leeway. Say his curfew is midnight and he is going to a movie. The movie is over at 10:30, and he can drop off his friends and get home in half an hour. You don't have to know exactly what he will be doing for the other hour.

With my boys, I did not want to tell them they could hang out on the street corner, but in truth, I actually didn't mind if they did because I knew I could trust them. By not asking, I didn't have to approve of everything they did, and by giving them a little leeway, I could allow them to exercise some judgment. Then, when something truly important came along, I knew

I could confront any one of my sons, ask him a direct question, and be sure he would give a truthful answer.

The world is not always fair, and certainly not always truthful. We took pride in the fact that our family was truthful and could trust one another. I complimented my sons on their truthfulness often. I spoke repeatedly to them (and to others in front of them) about how important truth is, and how proud I was of our family for being so truthful. I gave them something to take pride in and live up to, and they did.

I often spoke about the Friendshuhs and how important the truth was to them—how they always told the truth. It seemed to give my boys a sense of pride and certainly gave them something to look up to and be a part of.

One of the most difficult situations a parent and their child may face—once a parent knows that their child can be trusted to be truthful—is when he contradicts a person in authority, such as a school teacher. This is a very delicate situation. When I knew my son was telling the truth and the teacher was seeing it incorrectly, I did not challenge the teacher. I explained to my son that yes, I truly did believe and trust him, but life is not always fair. But that was many years ago.

Today, I feel some teachers and even some school districts have what I would consider radical ideas and I am not sure if they care if they are truthful or not. A parent should get to know their son's teachers or others in authority so they will know how to handle the situation.

One of the greatest dangers of TV and movies is how they glorify immoral values. Thieves or good con men are set up as heroes, trying to get away with whatever they can, trusting no one, and certainly not telling the truth. Even worse, the person who can be trusted to tell the truth is frequently portrayed as stupid, naïve, or simply as a nerd. This can be overcome by providing a child with more reinforcement of the values of truth and other virtues than the negative images of these values they receive from other sources.

Believe me, nothing will be of greater help in raising children than truth. It is worth all the effort and time that must be put into teaching it.

The Legend of Truth

If you would like to read my story on truth or read it to your children or grandchildren, see "The Legend of Truth" in the book Stories For All Ages.

Choosing a Babysitter

Choosing a sitter, even for a few hours, is not a choice to be taken lightly. Most importantly, parents must be sure the sitter knows their responsibilities, and will give their children the time and consideration they need. Getting someone who is known or someone recommended by another parent is perhaps the best alternative to a friend or relative.

Tell the sitter what you expect from them. Too many young babysitters watch television, talk on the telephone, and don't give their full attention to the children. I suggest parents should prohibit talking to friends on the phone or having friends over. If parents' views are somewhat the same as mine in regard to television, then they could also tell the sitter the television must stay off until the children are asleep.

The sitter also needs to know what house rules are important. Are the children allowed to run in the house or jump on the couch? Are any rooms off limits?

Parents should be sure to leave numbers where they (or someone they trust) can be reached. Having an up-to-date list of their child's doctors, close relatives and emergency contacts is also very important. When parents return, it's a good idea to discuss how everything went. Not only does this show interest and concern, but it will tend to keep the sitters on their toes. If children are old enough, parents should also speak to them about what they did and how things went. Even a three- or four-year-old can relate things.

Of course, having a regular babysitter who can be trusted, someone a child likes and is used to, is best. But there will still be times when a regular sitter will not be available, and a parent must look elsewhere. Even if parents know a sitter has a lot of experience with children, or they get a recommendation from someone who has a lot of experience with a particular sitter, they still really do need to do their own homework.

I vividly remember one instance about a babysitter and about truth. We had a regular sitter lined up, and at the last minute, she could not come. Her mother lined up another teenage girl to come in her place, and called to assure us this girl was a good and responsible sitter.

Our boys were about 7, 6, 5 and 2. We were gone for a few hours in the afternoon. When we returned, I noticed the mirror was bent on the car that had been left home. I asked the sitter and the boys about the bent mirror, and was told one of the boys had run into it. I was not comfortable with that explanation or with the very nervous, fidgeting attitude of my sons.

After we took the sitter home, we talked again with the boys. By this time they were crying because they felt so bad about telling their mom and dad a lie. This babysitter, who we trusted and represented to our children as being the person in authority, was telling those same children to lie. What a horrible situation for your children to be forced into. We comforted the boys, told them it was okay, and asked them to just tell us the whole story.

The babysitter had found the keys to the car and took our young children on a joy ride. She didn't even have a driver's license! We lived in the country, so her driving had been on gravel roads, with little or no other traffic.

Yet she still managed to sideswipe a mailbox with the mirror.

We called the babysitter, but she would not talk to us. I talked to the sitter's mother, and she seemed kind of supportive, yet I could sense an "Oh, well" attitude.

I called the mother who had recommended her. She apologized profusely and was truly sorry, but what could she do?

We were very lucky. The experience our children went through because they were forced to lie to us is something I will never forget, but I thank God it wasn't worse—our children could have been killed in an automobile accident.

Parents need to do the best they can, and any one of us could have gotten caught in this situation. If I had to do it over, I would question my friend more thoroughly. We found out she only knew her as a friend of her daughter. She really didn't know much about the girl herself, and only vaguely knew her parents. Even when parents gather all the information they can, they are still in the position of taking a minor chance or canceling their plans. When making that decision, it is important to realize the possible ramifications of using someone they know very little about.

After the phone calls, I did not forget the joy ride the

young sitter took with my boys. In an effort to make an impression on the sitter and perhaps avoid a situation like this in the future, I went to her home. I confronted her and her parents with a bill for the mirror and the extreme seriousness of what had taken place. I never did get paid for the mirror. I do not blame the young teenager but rather her parents. They obviously did not raise her properly.

Another thing to keep in mind is choosing a sitter who is not too close in age to the children. When I was in 4th or 5th grade, my parents hired a sitter who was in 7th or 8th grade. I remember her taking me into the bedroom and teaching me to neck. We only kissed and hugged. But talk about a potentially explosive situation! Bottom line, parents should choose a sitter with the utmost care and, if possible, choose one at least five or six years older than their children. That way, a senior in high school can still watch a sixth grader. By the time a boy is in seventh grade, he should no longer need a sitter.

Everything a child experiences has an effect, so make sure a babysitter knows what is expected. Even allowing children to watch things made especially for kids can have an adverse effect, as the following story shows.

Scary Things

Written by Jeanne

Even as an adult, I am still a big fan of animated children's movies. One year for my birthday, I wanted the Land Before Time video, which of course made my grown daughter chuckle.

*When **Finding Nemo** came out, I was there on its first day of release to get my coveted "2-disc Collector's Edition* *with Exclusive DVD Bonus Features." I couldn't wait to watch it, and wasn't disappointed. I loved it. The premise of the story was heart-wrenching, the animation was phenomenal, and the characters were extremely lovable, but I was most aware of the number of frightening scenes. Of course, when I was watching it, I had my two-year-old grandniece and grandnephew in mind. I wanted to get them a copy of this, but decided the violence was a little too much for them.*

When I told my sister this, she laughed because she had already purchased a copy for the twins. She hadn't seen it yet and was surprised at some of the scenes I described. However, she had an observation I had never thought of—the twins were too young to realize what was going on, so she was sure it wouldn't bother them. Since one of Regan's favorite videos was Jumanji, I had to believe my sister's observation was correct.

This premise held true for almost another year, then something changed. As the twins grew more and more aware of things, and learned new things at a phenomenal rate, they started to observe and absorb what was actually happening in these frightening animated scenes. It happened slowly, and no one was aware of it until Matt (now age 3) made it abundantly clear.

One day while riding in the car to go to a playground, Lonnie (my sister) and Debbie's mom, Helen, were talking about going somewhere at night, and Matt said, "No! Matt get killed." Lonnie and Helen were both shocked at his use of the word "killed," and thought they had heard him wrong. When they asked him what he'd said, they got the same response.

Since the kids are not exposed to anything else that could have given Matt an understanding of that word, they readily concluded the exposure to the violence in the animated videos had done it. Those scenes were no longer just splashes of color and loud music. They were now frightening, scary, and way too loud. The kids had shown a preference lately for more calm movies, but my sister didn't make the connection until Matt's remark.

Other fears started to manifest at the same time, including a fear of the dark or a fear of loud noises like thunder.

Our family, immediate and extended, now makes a concerted effort to screen everything before the twins are exposed to it, and it has started to make a difference.

What is very surprising is how difficult a task this has turned out to be. There is so much violence, even in things developed specifically for kids, that it has become a very time consuming effort to find appropriate material.

Needless to say, it's been well worth the effort.

Luke, Tim and Matt

My Child Isn't Feeling Well

Should I make him mind?

Giving advice in this matter is a lot easier than following that advice myself. Certainly, when a child is very ill, parents will want and need to pamper him and overlook things they may not overlook otherwise. I found it very difficult, if not impossible, to be hard on my son when I knew he wasn't feeling well. I do not expect it will be any easier for anyone else.

I just want to point out a few things, and then parents need to let their feelings and the situation dictate their response. I believe it does more good than harm to be overly protective and comforting to a sick child. But a child will pick up on this and might try to take advantage of it. Sometimes when my sons didn't want to do what they were told, they claimed they didn't feel well, like a bellyache. I tried to have some sort of distasteful medicine on hand for such occasions. It's amazing how miraculously they were cured when I reached for it.

If a child is really sick and it only lasts a few days, no one can go wrong overlooking many things and showering them with love and attention. It is with an extended illness that allowing him to get away with things can become a problem. Though a child may not be feeling up to par, a parent should consider making him mind during a long recovery time.

Some of the children who have the most difficult time doing what they are told are those who have gone through a long childhood illness. The parents (and perhaps everyone around them) allowed poor behavior during their illness. As harsh as it may sound, this does the child little good. If a parent is capable of being strict with their sick child, it will benefit him overall.

During an extended illness, if a parent cannot be as hard on their child as they perhaps should be, they will have joined the ranks of the many. Their compassion is truly understandable, but their child may have a difficult time later because of it.

On the other hand, if a parent can discipline him the same way they would if he were healthy (along with extra love and attention), their child will certainly benefit from their saintly efforts. No parent should be hard on themselves if they seemingly fail in this area. They just need to be aware of what they are doing, and do the best they can. They certainly can require their child to mind and still give him lots of extra love and comfort. Just keep in mind that even healthy children can be great manipulators.

When Daniel was about three, he came to me crying about something, and from the way he was carrying on, I thought he was really hurt. I picked him up, put him on my shoulder, hugged him, and patted his back. Although I could feel his little body sobbing, I happened to walk by a big mirror and notice the expression on his face. He was no more hurt than the man in the moon. He had gotten what he wanted and his face showed it.

How many times have you watched other children acting a certain manner, then when their mother comes, the child completely changes. Once my neighbor brought her boy Tom to play with my son Daniel. The two six-year-olds played together happily with little or no fighting. Tom didn't complain to me that Daniel wasn't sharing or he had taken something away, because he knew I would not tolerate either one of them complaining. So they worked things out between them and cheerfully played together all afternoon. When Tom's mother arrived to do some cleaning for me, Tom immediately complained to her. "Daniel isn't sharing, Daniel is annoying me, Daniel won't leave me alone, Daniel is being mean." He also went to her crying several times. He cried about things he would ignore if she were not there to listen.

I am not trying to pick on Tom's mother—I am sure Daniel manipulated me in similar ways. Even healthy children are absolute experts at manipulating their parents, so parents must be on guard and aware of this.

I was blessed because my children never had any illness lasting over a few days. For those short periods of time, no one can go wrong by letting their sick child get away with a few things. I hope I would have been able to handle things differently if one of my sons had been sick for several weeks or even longer; but perhaps not.

No parent can be faulted for being extra lenient with a sick child. They just need to be aware of the possible negative consequences in the long term.

I had trouble coming up with a related story, so I am going to share a true story that greatly affected how I raised my sons.

An Alaskan Six-Year-Old

When my first born was about a year old and my wife was pregnant with our second, we moved to Alaska.

I wanted to homestead, but the only homestead land available at the time was 50 miles from the nearest road. I assured my wife I would take good care of her and that I was capable of delivering our second child.

She would have none of it. These unreasonable women (Smile).

We met another homestead family who had come into Anchorage for supplies. They had their six-year-old son with them, and they told us a story about him.

Last winter, he had put up a stink about doing his chores. He was responsible for bringing the fire wood from the woodshed to the cabin. He had forgotten to do it, and when his father reminded him, he didn't want to.

It was about ten degrees below zero, with several feet of snow on the ground, and it was dark. Of course, it was almost always dark in Alaska in the wintertime. The fire in the cabin was warm, and being a normal six-year-old, he didn't want to go out in the cold if he thought he could get his dad to do it for him.

His father told him if he didn't carry his weight around the house he could pack up and leave. It seems his boy was a little strong-willed and answered, "Fine, I'll leave." He proceeded to get all dressed for the cold, went out into the dark, put on his snowshoes, and left.

His mother and father looked at each other in astonishment. They too lived over 50 miles from the nearest road.

Finally mom said, "Well?"

Dad said, "I'm going." He got dressed, put on his snowshoes, and followed his son's trail into the darkness.

About a mile down the trail, his son had stopped and built a fire. His father asked him if he could join him and warm himself.

They had a long man-to-man talk, and both apologized to each other. Then, under the Northern Lights, they returned to the cabin together.

Seeing his son run around in a breechcloth in forty-degree weather, and seeing him interact with his father I absolutely believed the story.

This six-year-old did something most modern-day men wouldn't have the guts or the know-how to do, and his father thought nothing of it. I made up my mind right then and there I would bring up my boys in the same manner.

And I did!

Starting School

Before my son went to the dentist for the first time, we played dentist at home. I had him wait in the waiting room, and then come in and sit on a big chair. Then I had him open his mouth wide, stuck my fingers in, and even took a piece of silverware and tapped his teeth. I tried to make conversation like I thought the dentist would and tried to give him a sense of what was to come. I did this with Daniel at about age three. It was a fun playtime, and he loved it.

This was so successful I used the same routine with going to school. I talked often with him about how great going to school would be. I did whatever I could to help build joyful anticipation and a positive attitude. We also played school and even practiced how it would be on the bus. I took a simulated roll call, assigned Daniel his seat, asked questions, and showed Daniel how he must raise his hand in order to be able to speak. We also talked about how some children might be mean or not particularly nice on the bus, or even in school itself. I told him this was wrong, and I did not understand it. I told him I was so proud of his brothers for never teasing or picking on others, and I knew I would be proud of him too. I laid out school clothes and talked with him about what he could and could not wear. I gave him choices of school appropriate clothes, but made it plain that regardless of what other students wore, he was going to wear appropriate clothing.

We maintained control, and required our son to respect us, himself, and his family by maintaining his appearance. We let him know he was a reflection of us and his family. Before he faced peer pressure, we began teaching him that he and his family operate under certain guidelines, regardless of what other children and their families do. If a child has an adequate sense of self-esteem, he should not feel the need to follow the crowd, but rather will be comfortable with himself and his choices.

When my oldest son Luke started school, he got on the bus carrying a briefcase. After school, we talked to him about his first day, and his first bus ride. He said some of the kids teased him about carrying a purse on the bus. We asked if this had bothered him, and he said no, because he wasn't carrying a purse—he was carrying a briefcase. Luke is the quietest and most reserved of my five sons; and yet, at this very young age, he had enough self-esteem and confidence that other children's teasing did not bother him.

A child is truly affected by all he experiences, and he will have some negative ones. We tried to keep the lines of communication open and tried to be of whatever help we could. We showed interest in his learning and gave him some of our time. We helped him with his schoolwork and his reading. Put his papers on the refrigerator or in another place of prominence, where he could see them. We praised, praised, and then praised some more. We tried to help him feel proud of what he was learning to accomplish. If a child likes school and feels good about what he is learning, he will do very well.

All of us are not able to choose our child's teachers, yet if a parent's time and their school allow it, I suggest they visit each of the teachers who may teach their child. If their school has two or three teachers for first grade, for example, they should talk to each one. Perhaps even talk to other parents whose children have had these teachers. If a parent can determine one is better suited to teach their child, and if their school allows this, they should request that particular teacher. Most schools, for obvious reasons, discourage this. Yet if parents show their interest and are persistent, oftentimes they may choose their child's teacher.

Whether or not a parent likes their child's teacher as a person or a teacher, they should show confidence towards that teacher. If they need to question their child's teacher or their methods, they should not do it in front of their child. In fact, it may even be best not to let a child know they are doing it. The teacher's methods may not be their methods; but they certainly do have value, and parents will help their child more by supporting the teacher's methods than by undermining their authority.

School should be something a child looks forward to, and if a child is encouraged, praised, and helped, he will want to be there. And reading will help him the most to enjoy school. I cannot overly stress how important being a good reader is. Parents should read to him often. Encourage him to look at books, and have lots of them available. And not just story books— have books that tell him about the wonders of life and the natural world. The **ChildCraft Encyclopedia** was always available to our sons, and they loved it. The encyclopedia opened up the lines of communication because it triggered questions and discussion. If a child has unlimited TV, he probably will not like books and school might be much harder for him. On the other hand, if he likes books and likes to read or is excited about being read to, he will become a good reader. As a good reader, school will be easy for him, and along with parents' continued support and interest, he will like school.

If parents find a good school, their main difficulty will not be with the school or the school's authority; but more likely with all the other children. Even if a child has a very good set of values and healthy self-esteem, he may still choose some friends who will not be good examples. Yes, perhaps a child can be a good example to them, but particularly at a young age, he should not be put in a situation that may be too difficult for him to handle.

When a child has a friend over, parents should pay attention to what is going on, and get a sense of what kind of child his friend is. They should talk with that friend's parents, and find out from others whatever they can about their family and family values. If a child gets involved with another child who perhaps does not possess a good set of values, he should be able to handle the situation within the school setting. He may even be able to handle most situations in an afternoon visit with a friend. But be careful about sleepovers, allowing a child to spend the night with a friend or have a friend stay overnight. A child could be more easily adversely influenced in such settings.

Most of the above was originally written over twenty years ago and many things have changed. Today, parents should be aware of what the school, or a child's teacher, is teaching about non-academic issues. I think parents should do whatever it takes to find out what their child's school is teaching or what the school policy is on things like biological boys using girls' bathrooms or locker rooms, or the like. They should talk to other parents and attend school board meetings. Most importantly, they need to talk to their children every day about what went on at school.

A child's values, work ethic, ability to handle responsibility, and healthy self-esteem will help him make the right decisions in life, in school or in whatever he chooses to do. He will not get these things from school. He must get them from his parents!

Dyed Hair

When Daniel was about 11 years old, he came home from visiting his mother with his hair dyed brassy blond. He is a brunette. I asked him if he wanted me to shave his head, or if he wanted to go to town and get a bottle of dye to dye his hair back to its normal color. He chose the dye. Perhaps he accepted my directive so readily because he knew his older brothers were not allowed to have earrings or tattoos. He knew I was the authority in the family, and he long ago had accepted that.

Friends and Peers

Interaction with other children is part of a child's development and can bring many positive and necessary results, yet this is the beginning of making a parents job a lot more difficult. As a child grows older, if he truly has good self-esteem, he will be able to interact with other children and yet remain above peer pressure. I have talked a little about peer pressure in the preceding chapter on starting school. I cannot emphasize enough the fact that everything a child experiences will have an effect. All his friends and other children he interacts with will also have an effect. It is extremely important that parents try to monitor who their child associates with whenever possible.

Even though our sons seemed to have the right type of friends, we tried to make sure they were not put in a situation none of them were capable of handling. We knew the easiest pitfall was to allow our son to stay overnight at a friend's house, because it is almost impossible to give continued direction during these long periods of time together.

The younger our sons were, the more influence we had over them. We worked hard during these early younger years, and we were able to coast when most families were having problems. Not only did we direct our sons to certain friends, we gave them direction on how to interact with those friends. As a child gets older, this will become more difficult; and he may even resent someone trying to choose his friends. We were very subtle in these efforts.

Another way we guided our sons towards certain friends was by setting standards and rules for our home. We choose what type of conduct or dress was allowed in our home or in our presence. That in itself probably weeded out some kids. Some weren't invited because my boys knew they wouldn't act appropriately; or if they did, they wouldn't be allowed to do as they wished. We remained firm and consistent on these points, and our son respected and accepted our rules. At some point in time, we did respect our son's choice of friends, but we never did allow him to do certain things because his friends were allowed to do them. We continued to enforce the fact that we, he, and his family have certain rules, responsibilities, and guidelines that do not change just because others seem to be acting differently.

Another thing we tried to do was to treat our son and his friends as we would treat other adults. We made sure our son felt important in his own home. When he brought a friend over, I introduced myself and shook his friend's hand. I spent a little time talking with his friend, just as I would do with another adult who came into our home. I also took the opportunity to compliment my son in front of his friend on something he had recently done. That seemed to make him proud of himself and his family.

If I had to discipline or have the kids quiet down, I didn't bark at them. I talked to them as I might talk to another adult, such as—"Daniel, you know when I am working on my computer you need to be more quiet. Must have forgot, huh?" "Daniel, you know you're not supposed to run in the house. You must have forgotten because you're having so much fun. I am counting on you to remember the rules."

Most children are not accustomed to being treated politely by adults. When I treated my son and his friends with respect, they respected me in return. I also did not scream or speak sharply to my son or his friends. I certainly talked sternly if needed but I did so in a calm, authoritative manner that showed respect for those who I was talking to.

It made even more of an impression when another adult came over and I introduced the adult to my son's friend. I did not fall into the trap or habit of treating children like second-class people, acting like they were not there, or that they didn't count.

We gave our sons the gifts of respect, self-esteem and family and it led to one of our greatest successes. My older four sons said they never experienced peer pressure. What a blessing this turned out to be, not only for us but for them as well.

Respect

One day, I went to pick up Daniel at school. He had only eight other first graders in his class. The kindergarten students were gone, and the first graders were all by the door getting ready to leave. I knew six of them, but hadn't met two of them. I reached out my hand and said, "You must be new here. I am Gary, Daniel's dad. What's your name?" They were a little embarrassed and looked at the floor; but they shook my hand, and it made them feel special. It made Daniel proud of his father, too; and even the slightly surprised teacher seemed pleased. We as adults just plain forget to treat children with the respect that they should have.

Me, Mark and Luke

Raising My Child Alone

Raising my fifth son, Daniel, alone for several years made me fully realize how blessed I had been to have a spouse there for both me and my first four sons. It also gave me a different perspective with regard to the primary child caregiver. I came to understand more fully how much of the burden their mother had shouldered at times. If I could do it over again, I would help her a lot more.

When raising Daniel, alone I was grateful and hopefully gracious for whatever help his mother was willing to give. At times this was difficult because I had certain routines and rules about things that were allowed or not allowed, I had some difficulties because his mother did not respect many of those routines and rules. Yet I only spoke positively, or not at all, about his mom. I also encouraged him to correspond with and spend time with her.

When Daniel got contradictory messages from his mother, I tried to talk to him about the differences between us. I tried to talk to his mother about this too. On the things she would not talk about or refused to respect my wishes on, I could only explain to Daniel that everyone is entitled to their opinion, but that I expected him to follow my routines and rules.

The contrast between raising my oldest four sons in a traditional two-parent family and raising Daniel by myself were very evident. In my traditional family, I was the breadwinner, the disciplinarian, and the authoritarian figure. I believe I was a very traditional father. I was the obvious head of our family, and the entire family looked to me for guidance and direction.

I spent a lot of time with my four boys and taught them many things. I also had the luxury of being able to teach them to be tough and endure the hurt or pain. If they needed additional comfort, they could always go to Mom. Yes, I too could comfort my sons, but it was much easier to play the role of the traditional man.

Because I wasn't with them continually, when I was there, they valued my time more. They listened more intensely, and they wanted to be with me as much as possible. I also did not have to be the one changing diapers, or cleaning up vomit, or rocking a sick child to sleep. I did not have to wash their clothes, teach them how to brush their teeth, or tie their shoes. I did not realize at the time how easy I had it.

Perhaps from their mother's point of view, she too was not aware of how easy she had it. All parts of parenting hold equal weight, and to shoulder just half of that weight truly is a blessing.

In my single parent family, I assumed all those roles and shouldered all the responsibility. Yes, Daniel still had his mother; but because she was not always there I had to assume all the roles. I had to be both mommy and daddy, so to speak.

I was very lucky, because as a rancher I could take my one-year-old son with me almost everywhere I went. As he grew older, keeping him with me became even easier. In addition, I was able to hire someone to help cook and clean, so I did not need to hire a babysitter or use daycare.

I did not mind the dirty diapers, the laundry, or the never-ending responsibility. I only had a lot of difficulty when Daniel was sick. It got to be almost more than I could handle when he was sick, and I too was sick.

At times like these, I asked for help from a neighbor who had a boy the same age as mine. They were a traditional family, and occasionally they would take Daniel or I would take their son, Tom. I saw to it that I had their son more than they had Daniel, but I never had to help them out when their son was sick. However, one time when Daniel and I were both sick, they all came up to my place and helped us get through it. If a single parent does not have neighbors or extended family like that, then I suggest they go out of their way to build a friendship with someone they can call on in times of great need.

Daniel's mother helped instill in him a deep faith, and I am grateful for that. She also has made other contributions to his life, but we do see some important things differently. She didn't say anything nice about me either. I just had to put up with that. She was very angry with me because I was awarded legal and physical custody of our one-year-old son. But when Daniel graduated from high school, she brought me to tears by telling me on the phone that I had done a good job of raising him.

Some advice for others out there

Raising a child alone may seem like an impossible task, particularly if a parent must work 40 hours a week to provide for themselves and their child. But remember, beyond the absolute necessities of food, clothing and shelter, nothing money can buy can provide anything that compares to the time spent with a child.

I have seen so many single parents, particularly mothers because they most often are the ones with the kids, overcompensate for their single income. They want to make sure their child has everything other children have, so they may deprive their child of the most important thing of all, their time. Perhaps they feel the need to prove to themselves, their extended families, or friends that they can do it.

To others, and possibly even to themselves, it may seem like they are doing a good job because the kids have most of the material things. Yet if the kids don't have time with that single parent, they are hurt. Often that hurt won't even be evident until the kids are older. Then one day the parent may have to ask themselves what went wrong. Why are my kids rebelling? Why won't they mind? Why are they so influenced by peers, and why won't they listen to me any more?

The sad part is when that happens, the parent still doesn't know why. They think they have given their kids everything. Society says they have given their kids everything. Society pats them on the back, and says, "You did such a good job as a single parent. You provided your kids with everything, and that sure wasn't easy for you." They continue making the same mistake with their younger kids, and society keeps encouraging families in the wrong way.

Nothing parents can give their children is more important than their time.

That is twice as hard for a single parent, but twice as important because the missing parent often isn't giving of their time either.

If a single parent has preschool children, and they can be home with them more by riding a bus and living in a much poorer neighborhood, then they should ride the bus and live in that neighborhood. They should not ever believe that the extra comforts money can provide will ever replace their time with their child. Any child needs his parent's loving time more than anything beyond the bare necessities of life.

A single parent should realize that they, too, will need help at times. There will be times when they come home from a long day's work and their son is sick. They are up with him most of the night and need to be with him the next day. Perhaps they are getting sick too. At times like these, they need extended family or a friend they can call upon. They can let that friend know that they can call upon them in similar circumstances.

If they are lucky, they can perhaps even call upon their child's other parent. It certainly will do no good if they get run down, sick, and can't function properly. Yes, their child comes first, but in order for them to care for and nourish him, they must take care of themselves too. If parents can get help, have them cook, clean, or do other chores or errands, so they have more time to take care of their child themselves.

Not only does a single parent need to provide their time and the necessities of life, but they still need to nourish and teach their son all he should know. If their son's other parent is absent, nearly absent, or lacks essential parenting skills, their job of teaching morals and values and applying discipline will be much more difficult. As a single parent, they are there alone, rarely getting a break, but neither does their child get a break from them. In a traditional family, he can go to the other parent. He also learns to feel more comfortable with each of the traditional parent's roles. In a single parent family, he may not know which role a parent might assume. He gets hurt, and one time you kiss it and make it better, and the next time you tell him it's nothing—go back out and play.

I worried so much about Daniel not having a mother and father together to raise him. But a very good and wise friend assured me that children are resilient. However, a child being raised by a single parent has the same needs and rights as any other child. It is just going to be twice as hard for the single parent to make sure they are fulfilling all those needs, and teaching him all that he has a right to be taught.

When it was especially hard, I kept reminding myself that it was not my son's fault that he did not have a mother and father together, it was our fault and whatever price had to be paid to make it easier for him, I needed to pay it.

Holiday on Ice

Written by Jeanne

As a single parent, the concerns I had about my daughter's activities when I was at work were monumental. When she was little, I was fortunate to have friends (with kids her age) to depend on, but as she got too old for sitters, my worry heightened.

Since she wasn't really into team sports, that wasn't the answer. So many of my friends simply left their children home by themselves. That didn't seem to be the answer either, at least for me. I tried to think of something that would truly interest her, and there was only one answer—ice skating.

We were fortunate enough to have an ice skating rink only a couple of miles from our home, so I took her and her friends there often. The first time she had on a pair of skates, she was about seven. She was remarkable. At first I thought it was just motherly pride, but other parents and even the rink manager commented on her abilities.

As we frequented the rink more and more, I couldn't just sit there, so I soon was zooming around the rink too (at a much more sedate level than the kids of course). It was really fun, and something we looked forward to.

With the constant encouragement of the professionals at the rink, Kim started taking lessons, which meant lots of practice. I thought she would soon tire of the routine, and want to go back to just skating, but she never did. She just couldn't seem to get enough.

As her proficiency increased, so did the need for more time on the ice. We even got up VERY early each morning so we could be at the rink by 5:30 or 6:00 am, so she could practice before school. This was beginning to become an expensive proposition, and one I was not sure I could handle.

Taking another part-time job was the only answer, but I did not want to be away from my daughter any more than I already was. We were already spending so many hours at that rink (before school, after dinner, weekends), and I was not willing to give that up. Then a miracle happened. I had helped institute a Biological Illustration class at the university I had attended, and that led to a part-time job illustrating for the Biology department. My prayers had been answered. It was easy to work on sketches at the rink, so our life could continue to grow. As Kim's skills increased even more, she entered competitions and shows, all of which required costumes. I made hers, which was really fun; but even that led to making outfits for others, and helping to make outfits for the shows.

All of this hard work and time came to fruition when Kim was too old for sitters. Her school was close to the rink, so it was very easy for her to take the bus after school to the rink, and I would pick her up there after work. Everyone there knew her, and watched out for her. She also made a lot of friends there who were obviously interested in the same things she was. It was wonderful.

I then took it a step further. I went to her school principal and counselor and asked if it would be possible for them to give her a last period P.E. class; and if they would then allow her to spend that hour at the rink instead of the school. They were so supportive that it surprised me. Now she was not only doing something she loved, had more time to do it, but was getting school credit. It all seemed to be too good to be true.

When I think back on all the time, extra work, and long hours, I wonder how we did it. I do remember at the time that people thought we were crazy, because there were times

I was exhausted (Not Kim, of course. She had energy to spare). Yet our memories (Kim's and mine) are of an abundance of joy. She even got to meet Scotty Hamilton, just before he went to the Olympics. I guess I can truly say that I felt very lucky to be such a part of my daughter's life during this time, and all that effort was not a monumental chore or burden. It was truly a "Holiday on Ice."

Kim's first year in school

Kim's favorite ice skating outfit

Stepparenting

Raising a child as a stepparent
or with a stepparent

I have been on both sides of the stepparent issues. Daniel's mother had four children ranging in age from 6 to 16. She trusted me and allowed me a free hand. She allowed me to teach her sixteen-year-old son to run a chainsaw and her twelve-year-old son to drive a tractor. She also allowed me to require her six-year-old daughter to take her turn at doing the dishes, even though she had to stand on a chair to do them.

The children accepted my guidance and rules because their mother completely supported me, and because I tried to be very sensitive to their needs. Whatever I taught or required, I did so in a manner that allowed the kids to take pride in their learning. I also tried to teach them things they wanted to learn. More importantly, all the time spent teaching or requiring the children to take on new responsibility was doubled by the amount of time I spent doing things with them that were fun.

Perhaps my job was a lot easier, and the children accepted me more readily, because they did not have their natural father in their lives. If their natural father had been part of their lives, little would have changed on my part. I would have made it plain that I was not trying to take his place and was supportive of their contact with him. The most important thing was for me to give of my time and of my love.

When Daniel was about eight years old, Jeanne came into my life. Now I was on the other side of the stepparent issues. Most of my parenting responsibilities became much easier. Daniel had a new friend, and I had someone who was a much better nurse than I. She was also very good at helping him with school projects, birthday parties, and the like. She was much better at those hugs and taking care of injuries. My job as a parent became much easier, and Daniel has benefited greatly.

From my experience, if there are difficulties, I think the natural parent might have a more difficult time. Methods and approaches to raising children should be discussed beforehand and, for the children's sake, should be decided on and managed as consistently as possible. The natural parent should examine very closely if they are capable of giving the stepparent all the support that is required. The stepparent should be given support, but at the same time, the stepparent should accept that where consensus cannot be reached, the final decision on any course of action should be made by the natural parents.

Know that children will benefit greatly by being in a two-parent family. Just keep the lines of communication open between the two of you. And most importantly, always outwardly support each other.

The Birthday Party

It was a crisp January day, and Daniel's birthday was only a week away. At the time I didn't remember much about his past birthdays (kids, something to eat, the usual), but I knew this one was going to be different. Jeanne had come into our lives and this year was special.

Daniel was really into football, so she made that the theme. That in itself was something new for me—a theme. I just thought a party was a party. Was I ever wrong! First came the invitations, which she made on her computer (she's a very creative lady). They were miniature works of art, complete with football players, goal posts, and a fun poem inviting Daniel's friends to come and celebrate with him. Even the envelopes had footballs on them, and Daniel was so excited he couldn't wait to get to school to pass them out.

There, of course, was the predictable Denver Broncos tablecloth, plates, cups, and napkins. That was no surprise, but it was just the beginning of a very special day, and some very special memories.

I came down one morning and Jeanne was sitting at the kitchen table, which was covered with toys, treats, trinkets, bags, ribbons, and miniature paper footballs with the kids' names on them (another computer creation). As the bags got filled to overflowing, she somehow folded them to create this fan-like top, secured it with a ribbon, and pasted footballs all over the bags, one for each child. They were then placed on a ledge by the front door so the kids could see them when they came in. When Daniel came home from school that day, his excitement was apparent.

Our house was inundated with Bronco colors, as blue and orange balloons, streamers, and banners filled the whole place. She swirled together orange and blue ice cream and re-froze it, and had fresh oranges with blue candy cane sticks as straws.

I had been commissioned to plan all the activities, and with all that was going on around me, I took my job seriously. I'd planned indoor activities, outdoor activities, easy games, skill games, sports games, and even a horse racing game I'd invented. I made sure each child would win something and have a fun time.

Even the cake was different. It wasn't a square cake with a football drawn on it. It was a football—really shaped like a football, complete with the laces, and green coconut grass all around it. Daniel's little face just beamed, and he couldn't stop thanking her. But believe it or not, the best was still to come.

Each night we watched as she sketched away on all these 8½ by 11 sheets of paper. We kept asking what she was doing, but she just smiled and said it was a surprise. I can't remember why, but I was gone all day, and Daniel was in school. When we came home, we were speechless. There, taped to our front bay window, was a life-size picture of one of Daniel's favorite Denver Broncos football players, Terrell Davis wearing his number, 30.

Daniel could not believe his eyes, and couldn't stop talking. "Wow! Did you do that? How'd you do that? I can't believe it. Wow! Thanks." He couldn't seem to calm down. A sheet of plastic lay over the picture, and of course Daniel asked what it was for. Well, now for the last surprise.

Jeanne produced a pile of lifesize paper footballs, each one with a guest's name on it. Instead of playing Pin the Tail on the Donkey, Daniel and his guests were going to be able to play Pin the Football on the Running Back. I'd never seen his little face light up so bright or his eyes become so big.

The party was a huge success. The kids were excited as they entered and saw their bags of surprises on the side. They loved all the games and the food, but the hit of the party was Terrell. They ran straight to him when they got there, and couldn't stop asking Daniel where he got it. He beamed with pride as he told them. Then chaos erupted when they each got their own football to pin on. What fun!

We were exhausted by the end of the day, and of course the house looked like a mini cyclone had passed through. But as I looked at Daniel's excitement and smile, I knew we wouldn't forget this day for a long time. As everyone started to do their share of cleaning up, I headed over to take down Terrell. I was stopped in my tracks by an emphatic "No" from both Jeanne and Daniel. It seems Terrell was here to stay, part of our family. He was moved to a place of honor on Daniel's bedroom door, and remained there for many years.

Daniel's football birthday party

My Child the Person

All children are unique unto themselves, even prior to their birth. I could not believe the differences between my sons. My wife and I soon realized that each of our boys was a unique individual. Although we could guide and train them, they each had their particular way of adapting that guidance and training. My oldest son, Luke, was always very reserved, gentle, and even passive, whereas Tim was daring and anything but passive. Matt was tough and most always happy, and Mark was a thinker. We taught them all the same lessons, but at times, we had to use slightly different methods because of their distinct personalities.

We let each boy know we recognized, loved and respected their individuality. We helped them feel good about themselves, and never compared them to other children or their brothers. I also tried to make sure I had some one-on-one time with each boy, even if it was only an hour or so. When each son turned six, I took him on a weekend trip with just the two of us. This turned out to be so special that when they became fathers, they did the same thing with each of their children.

If one of our boys had some personality traits or tendencies that were not in his own best interests, we worked on helping him overcome those things. While it is not okay to allow a child to be weak and afraid, it is perfectly all right for them to prefer non-physical things and be more reserved. Remember, a child is an individual. He is different from his parents, his siblings, and from all those who have come before him.

We always took time to recognize our son and his presence, even when bringing adults into the setting. We tried to take the time to show an interest in what he was interested in, and we talked to him to find out how he felt about things and the world around him. We started these things with each of our sons when they were very young. We started them even before we felt he was aware of what we were doing. Certainly by the time each of our boys was two or three, they were aware of our attention and interest. We taught each of our boys all we felt they should know, but we did not force them to be something they weren't. I did however tell my boys the story about the Alaskan six-year-old (shared on page 133), and they all wanted to stay out all night alone in the back pasture when they were six.

All children are individuals, but they look up to their parents for guidance. Take them and their uniqueness, and help mold them into all they are capable of being.

The Rodeo

When my boys were 11, 10, 9, and 6, we lived on a farm and had cows and calves. A neighbor and friend of ours was a clown for a children's rodeo, and he kept telling my sons they should get their dad to build some chutes so they could ride calves.

Finally I gave in. We built a chute and gave the boys instructions on how to ride a calf. We put a calf in the chute and practiced letting him out. We also tried to soften up the ground a little for the boy's eventual fall. Matt and Tim wanted to go first, but I thought the oldest should be given that privilege. Luke said he wanted to do it, but thought it would be okay if Tim went first. Although Mark was only six, he watched and thought all three of his brothers were crazy. With my neighbor there acting as the rodeo clown, I helped Tim get on the back of a 250-pound calf. He put his hand under the rope and said he was ready. When we opened the door, the calf bolted out, took two enormous jumps into the air, and Tim went flying. He came down and landed with his face in the dirt, but jumped right up, smiling. After all, this whole thing was mostly his idea.

Luke settled down on the calf's back and took a grip. When we opened the chute, the calf bolted out and jumped into the air. Luke slipped down under the calf and didn't let go of that rope. The calf's hooves came up and kicked him in the stomach. When we got to him, he was bleeding, and his stomach wall had been ripped enough that I had to push things back in. My neighbor ran to the house and called the doctor's office, letting him know we were on the way in. Luke was not bleeding a lot, but the wound was substantial. They took him into the doctor's office immediately and gave him several stitches. He didn't cry, but he didn't watch either. The doctor told him he would have a nice scar to remember his rodeo days by.

Luke said, "My rodeo day!"

When we got back home, Matt took me aside and asked

me when he would get his turn. I couldn't tell him what I was thinking, so I just said, "Sorry, son. Mom won't allow it." Actually, Mom might have shot me had I allowed it.

Matt never did get to try riding calves, and none of the boys ever tried it again, but Matt did get his turn at stitches. He was riding his bike down a hill on a gravel road next to a barbed wire fence. Dad had ridden there with him before. But this time he was trying to see how fast he could go. He took a spill and ripped his leg open on the barbed wire. He had cowboy boots on, and by the time he walked about a quarter mile home, one boot was almost completely full of blood. He was not crying, and just came in and told his Mom he had taken a spill. Mom loaded the boys into the car and took him to the doctor. While the doctor put in about 25 stitches, Matt sat up on his elbows and watched him do it. The doctor told him that he would probably grow up to be a doctor, because most kids, and adults for that matter, didn't like watching such things.

Besides learning that each of my sons were unique individuals, I did learn something else from all this. Twenty-five years later, when Daniel wanted to ride sheep at a local rodeo, called mutton busting, I wouldn't let him do it. I didn't encourage bike riding on hills near barbed wire fences either.

Postscript

This story does speak of my son's uniqueness, but it also speaks of their willingness to try anything Dad says is okay. So be careful what you say is OKAY..... Smile!

The Opposite Sex

Teaching and Talks

When children are very young, they are blind to gender. It is up to their parents to teach them to show consideration for the differences.

For instance, on our ranch, my boys just went potty wherever they found themselves. They had to be taught it was inappropriate to do in front of girls.

One hot day, the neighbors were visiting with their three-year-old daughter. The kids wanted to take a dip in a small pool. Since Daniel was only about two and a half, we thought nothing of putting the two children into the pool together without their clothes on. At some age, of course, this is no longer appropriate. This is something for parents to determine, perhaps differently for each child, depending on their level of maturity.

Children should never be taught their bodies are anything but good, beautiful, and natural; but at a certain age, they need to be taught the difference between the sexes and appropriate respect for the opposite sex.

I also believe it is appropriate to teach little girls to be kinder and gentler, and to teach little boys to be tougher (try not to cry when it hurts); but that is a matter of opinion and I do not feel it is necessary.

Teaching about the opposite sex really comes into play when a child begins school. My five-year-old son had already begun acting differently around girls by the time he started kindergarten. He blushed more easily, tended to be kinder, and shared more with girls than with boys. He picked this up without me specifically teaching him anything. The schools have no business teaching any of this. It is up to parents to teach these things.

Now, I have never raised girls, and can not judge if the following suggestions would work with girls as well as it seemed to work with my sons.

Sex is a part of life and, as such, should be in normal conversations. A little boy should be able to ask about his body when he is very young, and should be able to tell you if his penis hurts. When he sees two dogs breeding or has a young pup crawl on his leg and rub against him, a parent should be able to explain it at his level if he asks what is going on.

Children have no inhibitions and do not feel the least bit uncomfortable talking about sex or their bodies. Parents may make them uncomfortable by their own actions, reactions, or discomfort. But they should not give their children those hang-ups.

Some of my sons' formative years were spent on a farm or a ranch and lived around livestock, so the reproductive functions were common. I talked to them about the baby calf being inside of the cow, and how it got there. These were not difficult subjects with my young sons.

When my boys were quite young, they would occasionally fiddle around with themselves in the tub.

When they were really young, I said nothing.

When they were about five years old, I told them they should scrub down there very well, but not to dwell there.

"Why?" was often their honest, direct question. I answered, "God has given you that part of your body for going potty and for being a father."

"How?" This was a little easier for me with my youngest because he grew up around bulls and cows. "That is how you put the seed in."

Stop whenever the questions stop.

If your child continues asking "How?" then you should continue.

"Your penis gets hard. Then you put it in your wife's vagina to put the seed inside of her. It meets up with an egg inside of her and that grows into a baby." None of my boys at this young age pursued this any further than that.

In case a child continues questioning, a parent could go a little further. "That is why it feels good when you touch and scrub down there. God made it feel good for bulls or men so they would want to put the seed in the cow or the woman."

It's much easier to do this when they are very young. Build a comfort zone.

I just relaxed and talked to them as if I were talking about anything else, be it gardening, playing, or whatever. It is all natural, and I just considered it as such.

I will admit that as my first four boys got older, the subject became a little difficult for me. Now, as a man of many seasons, I find this no different from any other subject. With my fifth son Daniel, who I had when I was 48, I had no difficulty at all talking about everything and anything.

At what age a parent chooses to have a specific sex talk is important; and I believe that in the beginning, it is best if fathers talk with their sons and mothers with their daughters. Each of us matures at different ages, and parents should be able to assess their child's level of maturity. If a parent is to make an error in their assessment, I believe they are better off erring on the side of having the discussions with their child at too young an age.

When I decided to have that first detailed talk on the subject, all my groundwork had been done. So when I wanted to have a talk about sex, it was no big deal.

I usually started by asking questions about how much they knew. Usually because of my early groundwork and their exposure to livestock, they pretty much knew the physical aspects. If they were reluctant to tell me how much they actually knew, I would go through the basics.

Then I followed up with something like this: "We as human beings must learn to be in control of our wants and desires. As a young child, we may want to play with knick knacks, but we know we are not allowed to do it, so we don't. When we are in a store, have no money, and are very hungry, we may want that candy bar, but we know we can not just take it. We like soda, but we know if we drank all we wanted, it could make us sick. We do not feel like getting up in the morning, but since we are in charge of our bodies, our mind makes our body get out of bed.

"God has given man a very strong physical desire to be with a woman, not only to assure the continuation of mankind as a species but also to allow an intimacy between a husband and a wife that forms a special bond. Our physical desires and maturity start very young, and as a part of this process, we will often get excited and get an erection. We may get it in our sleep, or from riding on a bumpy bus, or from seeing some picture or girl who looks nice to us.

"This is all a natural part of maturing, but we can not let nature or these feelings take control of our life. When a dog or a bull gets excited and sees a cow or another dog, he goes and tries to insert his seed into her. We, as human beings, can not react to those kinds of instincts. When we get mad or angry at another human being, we can not just slug him; and when we feel these sexual desires, we can not just act upon them. It is part of being in control of oneself.

"We should not continue to touch ourselves or play with ourselves down there whenever we feel like it, because we must teach ourselves to be in control and not let our bodily urges be in control. If once in a while your body releases semen in your sleep, or you touch yourself and it comes out, that is nothing to be ashamed of. You are not ashamed of eating; but if you eat too much, lose control, and can't stop eating, then you could get fat, and that is a problem. You must be in control of your body, so try the best you can not to fiddle around with yourself. Save this special gift for a time in your life when you are a husband and perhaps a father. Make absolutely sure you keep this special gift private, and you do not goof around with other boys or girls."

The Bull

For those of you not familiar with the carrying on of bulls and cows, I'll give you a short lesson. When cows are in heat, other cows and calves will mount them; and occasionally the cow in heat will mount another cow. I suppose nature has caused this so the bull can see it from a long way off and come running.

Normally when the bull arrives, the cow will be coy for a while. The bull will follow her around, sniffing her whenever he can. Right after he sniffs her, he will often raise his head, curl up his nose and raise his upper lip and show his teeth.

One time, when Daniel was a little over three and was visiting his mother, they took a trip through the country. They were going somewhere in the car with a few of her suburban lady friends. As they were driving by some pasture land, they came upon a stop sign and a small herd of cows right in the corner of the fence line. One of the cows was in heat and was being followed in a small circle by a bull. Just as they stopped, the bull got a good whiff, lifted his head in the air, curled his nose, and showed his teeth.

Three-year-old Daniel points his finger out the window at the bull and says, "Look, Mommy, the bull is smiling!"

Girls in Colorado

When we lived in Colorado, our ranch was ten miles from our nearest year round neighbor, and I was a guide and an outfitter.

Not only did I take people on elk and deer hunts, but we had people come out that we took fishing, camping, and riding.

The boys got up at 3 am, helped saddle horses for an elk hunt or other preparations, and sometimes they came along as a wrangler.

One time we had a whole pack of Girl Scouts come to the ranch—at least 12 of them. They were all at least freshmen in high school, and most were a little older. My older three boys were in 8th, 7th and 6th grades, but they were all tall for their age and worked like men. They gathered the horses, saddled them, rode in front and behind the string of girls, and helped them handle their horses.

The girls were really impressed, smitten even! Some of them even kept in contact with the boys by mail for the next year or so. At that time, we had no computers and, thank goodness, no telephones.

Mark, Luke, Tim and Matt

Home School

I did a little schooling at home but not what most would consider homeschooling. My boys attended traditional schools, some public and some private. But because I thought it was critical, I went out of my way to teach a few things myself, like economic classes.

In Daniel's case I started with the basics, and showed him how to handle a checkbook and set up a budget. I told him he could decide if he wanted to strictly follow a budget, but in any case, he should always keep track of where his money went.

I took extra time to explain credit cards. I emphasized how many people get into trouble with credit card debt. I told him he should never pay any interest on any credit card. In fact, all his debts should be paid on time.

I told him I tried for years to get by without having a credit card. But when I tried to rent a car, I found out I could not do so without one. In today's world, a credit card is almost a necessity, but paying interest on balances is not.

As a young person just starting out, he also needed to know a bad credit rating can take up to ten years to get corrected. I shared how I established good credit.

Once I had saved up to make a thousand-dollar furniture purchase, I asked the seller if I could charge it. When I was told no because I had no credit, I offered to pay him the thousand dollars up front if he held the cash for a week. He then could sell me the furniture on credit and pay it off a week later. I did get a receipt for the thousand dollars though! He agreed and I had established credit.

Other parents may have other topics—everything from shop class to chemistry to literature to math—if they feel their schools aren't handling these subjects well. They should make it their business to find out what their son is learning, and do their best to give him the background they feel he needs to be a successful adult.

We covered more, but you get the idea.

At the time my boys were in school, they were still being taught American History and Civics in a way I was comfortable with. Today it seems that most schools no longer teach civics and if they teach history at all, it is often biased against America. If that is the case parents should teach it the right way at home.

For example, I strongly believe our children need to be grateful they are Americans and they need to know how important free speech and the other things our founders gave us are. They also need to know how our government works.

Whatever a parent believes, it is up to them to protect their children from indoctrination or worse. It is up to them to make sure their children are being taught what schools should be teaching. Either they should teach it themselves or find a different school or homeschool.

The School Secretary

My fifth son, Daniel, went to a private school for his first six years. Bethesda was a small school and the school secretary, who had been there for many years, got to know all the kids on a personal level. She often said what a great kid Daniel was, but what impressed her the most was that, in all her years of being around children, she had never seen a happier child. She was also impressed by the fact that as a fifth and sixth grader, he always seemed to be helping out younger students.

I took a story I had written, "The Bear," to read to his second or third grade class. They loved it and Daniel beamed with pride. Afterwards he introduced me to several of his classmates and showed me around.

He was in several plays and other school activities. Everyone knew everyone else and the teachers and school secretary were always there. We even stayed friends with them all for many years.

One of the great advantages of a very small school.

Fighting

When it came to fighting, my boys and I had several discussions. I actually learned from them in this regard. I was a country boy who had gone to an inner city, all-boys' school, and I had a tough time there. I did go on to become a Golden Gloves boxer and was proud of my abilities. I wanted to teach my boys to be able to defend themselves, but my wife begged me not to. Out of respect for her wishes, I never taught them to box or to defend themselves. They were also country boys going to an inner city all-boys' school, yet none of them had any problem.

I do think it is very important to talk with children about bullies and to make sure they don't bully others even a little. As for fighting, I told my boys to just walk away, and that advice seemed to work well for them. It also helped that they were not easily influenced by peer pressure and had healthy self-esteem. Perhaps the fact that there were three boys, all each one year apart, helped the situation. My number four son, who was not in school with his brothers, did have a couple of instances where he needed to physically defend himself.

The important thing here is that if a child is taught

to box or defend himself, a parent should be absolutely sure he will not abuse his ability.

I believe three out of four of my older boys would not have misused boxing or self-defense skills. Perhaps none of them would have needed that knowledge. I would have been more reluctant to teach my son,Tim, because of his temper. Yet somewhere along the way he learned, and did get into a couple of altercations. He even got a reputation for being able to defend himself. Bottom line is, if the particular child feels a need, he will find a way to learn; or he may come for advice. A parent will have to decide on an individual basis whether to provide him with any instruction.

The last time I ever laid a hand on any of my older three boys was when Tim hit Matt in the face with a closed fist. Had I taught my boys to box, I'm not sure whether that would have helped or added fire to their conflict. I had told them many times that if they ever got into a fight with each other, they were not allowed to hit one another in the face. Tim lost his temper and gave Matt a black eye.

I did not really lose my temper, but I acted like I did. I grabbed Tim by the shoulders and threw him over the couch, sounding very angry. I threw him to the floor and acted terribly mad. I said through my teeth, "How would you like it if I lost my temper at you?" Then I told him to get up, and I would knock him on his ass.

Because of my previous groundwork, Tim respected me and did not get up. We smile about it today because he felt he was being good to his father. With Tim's 6'5" and 200 pounds size, youth and vigor, he certainly felt he could handle the situation. We older, more experienced men know the actual, very different truth. The most important thing, however, is it never even came close to that.

After having come in second in the upper Midwest Golden gloves boxing tournament (at about age 17), I remember a time when my father punished me physically for something; and for a short moment, I doubled up my fist and faced him. He looked at me, and I looked at him. Then I turned and walked away. At the time, in my youthful mind, I too thought I was being kind to him. Now, in my maturity, I realize he could have very easily handled the situation. The reason for sharing this is to show that both my father and I had done enough groundwork that our sons respected us enough to back off. Once more, pay a price early and reap the rewards later.

This perhaps is a time to share something that had a profound effect on my direction in raising children. I had a teenage friend, also a Golden Gloves boxer, who told me he was thinking of beating up his father. That incident led me to a basic belief that I always kept in my mind. If any of my sons ever turned on me or would not do as he was told I would just throw him out.

My son could make a mistake, say he was sorry, make the same mistake again and again and again, and I would continue to forgive him and try to do the best I could. But if my son had ever said there was no way he was going to do what he was told and I could not make him, then I would tell him to sleep on it; if he felt the same way in the morning, then he could pack his bags and go live on his own.

This may sound harsh, but I think letting a child do whatever he wants, regardless of what a parent tells him, is unacceptable. If a parent has absolutely no control, it is probably better for their son to be on his own. Maybe he will realize how good he really had it.

This is extreme, but some parents face this situation. If at all possible, a parent should not let this happen in their family. If they pay the price early, while their son is young, the teenage years will be happy ones for everyone.

As far as fighting with one's siblings goes, rules and guidelines are a must; but as the following story illustrates, sometimes just having a parent there to diffuse the situation is all that is needed.

Tim's Moccasins

Written by Tim

I know that time and memory are strange things. I'm 37, but I don't feel so different than when I was a child. I look at my son, almost 13 now, and I can remember what I was like and much of what I hoped and dreamed and thought about when I was that age.

Not everything, of course, but certain things. Moments; images; specific incidents; bits of conversations, many of the daily interactions with Dad, Mom, and, of course, my brothers. I wonder what bits and pieces my son will take with him into adulthood, what events will shape his personality and belief system. What things will be burned forever into his psyche, what things will simply pass him by and be forgotten?

I don't recall exactly how old I was, definitely older than eight but younger than twelve; Dad was going through his

"Native American" phase (of course, since it was the '70s, we called them Indians). There was some semi-mystical mumbo jumbo about animal totems and the universe as a circle that I don't recall much about at all, but when he had the hides from his annual deer hunting trips cured, that was interesting. We could make all sorts of cool and fun things out of natural deer-hide. The moccasins I recall as my particular favorite (I wish I could forget the breechclout). My brothers and I wore our homemade moccasins everywhere one summer, and of course, my original pair soon wore out.

I had watched Dad make the first pair, and I had a pretty good idea on how to go about it. Even as a kid, I'd always been good with my hands. Building things, figuring out how stuff worked, taking things apart and putting them back together was something I have been doing for as long as I can remember.

Making moccasins was easy, as it turned out; the heel was the only tricky part. Getting the sole to fold up and into the seam behind your heel so that it stayed put, didn't give you a blister, and was at least marginally water & mud proof. I was particularly happy with the way I figured out and finished the sole-heel tuck. It looked just like the book said it should. I showed them off to my brothers and, of course, they wanted to make their own too.

No names, (to protect the innocent!) but one of my brothers was so intent on getting his done quickly, that he ignored the tricky heel-sole fold altogether and just left a hole there where the sole and upper came together behind the heel. Imagine a floppy sandal with a very wide heel strap. I tried to explain how the way he did it was wrong, but he didn't care.

With all the earnestness of a pre-adolescent who knows

better, I tried reasoning with him. I explained the need for the tuck. I showed him the illustration in the book, the heel of his old moccasins. I even offered to do it for him. He ignored all my instruction efforts, he refused to acknowledge my direction, and he wouldn't even let me do it for him. He wanted a new pair of moccasins, he wanted to make them himself, and he didn't care if it was right or not, as long as he could wear them.

I was incensed. I knew the correct way. I had tried to explain, I had tried to help. How could he not care about doing it correctly? I had read the directions and looked at the drawings. I had pondered. I had experimented with a couple ways of 'folding' and now I had it all figured out. Here I was generously offering the benefit of my learning and experience. How could anyone be so ignorant and not even care?

How could he blithely ignore the evidence in front of his face, the illustrations so clearly showing how it was supposed to look? His moccasins didn't look like the pictures!

He simply said, "It isn't wrong. I'm doing it my way." By this time, I was getting mad; after a few more minutes of arguing about it, I was yelling at him. I was absolutely beside myself; I clenched my fists, ready to pummel him into submission. I would beat sense into him somehow! He just had to see it my way!

Fortunately, Dad came by to see what the ruckus was about.

I screeched, "HE'S DOING IT WRONG!"

My brother shouted, "NO I'M NOT, AND BESIDES, I DON'T CARE!"

Dad looked at me, he looked at the instruction book, he looked at the moccasin under construction in my brother's hands. He let me go on for a while about how it was supposed to be done. He let me show him the pictures in the book and how mine looked exactly like the ones in the book. Then he pulled me aside and asked me the question I will never forget:

"Why do you care if he does his wrong? Why does it matter to you?"

I sputtered; I choked. It was like having cold water dumped on my head.

"Uh... Well, because dirt and mud and stuff will get in, they'll leak, and he'll have blisters!"

"They're his feet, not yours," was Dad's calm reply.

"Ummm...well....because they'll wear out faster because the seams will unravel!"

"Well, they're his moccasins, aren't they?" was the reasoned response.

The last thing I could come up with was, "Because he'll want me to fix them for him later!" I was momentarily proud of this one. Of course it affected me. I was going to have to bail him out when his crummy moccasins failed!

"Do you mind doing that?" asked Dad. "Weren't you going to help him anyway?"

"...Ummm...no...Yeah, I guess so..." I mumbled. Dad was right. I wouldn't mind helping him fix them or even make a new pair. I didn't mind fixing things for others. Heck, at that age I was happy, tickled pink even, whenever anyone asked me to fix things for them. I loved doing it, and it made me feel great.

So in a few minutes, I went from frothing, irrational, righteous anger to the happy knowledge that before too long my brother would come crawling back to me for help, and he finally would acknowledge my superior wisdom and ability.

Guess what? It never happened. My brother was perfectly happy with his 'incorrect' moccasins for as long as we kept making and wearing them. And I learned a valuable lesson about human nature, educating the ignorant and the tyranny of good intentions.

Luke, Tim and Matt

Drugs and Booze

Drugs are a subject I am not very qualified to give advice on, but maybe I do have something to offer. I worked like a man when I was between 7th and 8th grade; and when the men I was working with had a beer, my father allowed me to have one too. I treated my boys the same way.

I never could understand the other boys who would bend over and hold their breath until they fainted, or drink something that tasted awful just to get a buzz. I drank beer because I liked it; to this day, I still do not like hard liquor. I also intensely dislike the feeling of losing control. On many a New Year's Eve, I stopped drinking because I felt myself starting to lose control. I just love life too much to want to escape from it. Maybe that is the key here. I am very proud of the fact I never even tried marijuana, and never wanted to. Yes, like most every other child, I did try a cigarette or two, but how most people get by those first few, I'll never know.

The only times I ever felt a buzz, I was doing something physical like playing volleyball and drinking beer like it was water.

I will never forget one New Year's Eve when we were at home doing just that, and it got away from me. We had a crowd there, so you'd get to play volleyball for a while, and then you'd play cards until your next turn on the volleyball court. The volleyball play made you thirsty, and playing cards provided the opportunity to quench that thirst. When the evening was over, my older four boys pointed and laughed at their father—seeing him for the first time not really able to stand up very well.

If my children liked beer and wanted a sip, I gave it to them. On our wedding anniversary, we got the champagne out and gave each of the boys, regardless of their age, a small glass of champagne. I think, in general, that it is very important not to give conflicting messages. If you are going to drink a beer, it is unrealistic to think your seventeen-year-old son will not want to have a beer. If you give your children healthy self-esteem and they are happy and love themselves and life, they are not going to want to escape from it. More importantly, they are not going to be coerced by their peers to do something they would not normally do.

When my oldest son graduated from high school, I allowed him to have his friends over and I let them have beer. I took all the car keys, and no one was allowed to leave until morning. Perhaps this was not a wise decision, and I probably should have checked with the other boys' parents and did not. I did have a close enough relationship with my son to know what he told me was true. He said if the other boys had not come to our house, they would have gone somewhere else to drink beer. Some may take issue with my response, yet I could have actually saved a life. I joined the boys, and not one of them got drunk in front of an adult. We all had a good time, and no one drove while under the slightest influence of alcohol. Most importantly, none of my sons ever had an alcohol problem.

I have very little experience with drugs and children. To my knowledge, only one of my five sons ever tried marijuana. I am convinced that one or two of them never did; but all of them respected me, my views, and themselves too much to let me know. If I have anything to offer, it would have to be that if a child feels loved, is happy, has healthy self-esteem, is not affected by peer pressure, and truly loves life, I do not believe he will ever have a problem. Parents can give their child these things if they put in the effort. It is not easy. It takes a lot of work and a lot of time; but I think if parents stop a moment and reflect upon it, they will realize that whatever it takes would most certainly be worth all the effort.

Jamie

The summer Mark was in Australia, I was home on the ranch alone, and my brother asked if he could send his sixteen-year-old son out for a month. It seems he had gotten into some kind of trouble with drugs, and my brother figured a month on a ranch might do some good for his suburban son. I said he could come, but he would have to work and I couldn't pay him very much.

Like his father, Jamie was extremely competitive and a very good athlete, but he had never done any amount of physical work before. I taught him to ride a horse, shoot a gun, drive a jeep, run a chainsaw, and work like a man.

Once we were up on the mountain putting in miles of fence. He looked down at the blisters on his hands and said, "I have never worked so hard in my life.

"And I love it!"

We started early in the day so we could end our work day by early afternoon. Often we would go swimming at the rocks, but almost every day, after swimming or work, we would look at each other and say "Football!"

In our free time, we did a lot of shooting, playing poker and other card games, and other games, but our favorite was a football strategy game I invented. Jamie loved it! We both enjoyed our free time together, and were always telling each other how we were going to kick the other's behind.

When his month was about over, he was trying to decide if he wanted to stay on for a while.

We talked about it, and I offered to double his $25 a month salary (smile), and let him shoot all the shells he wanted.

About that time we started talking about basketball, and he told me how good he was. Soon he said, "Lucky you don't have a hoop and a court, because I'd kick your butt."

Now I was 45 or 46, and he was 16, but I was also 6'3" and he was only 5'10".

I said, "I'll tell you what. I'll make you a bet. If I beat you, you agree to stay on for the rest of the summer, and I'll double your wages. If you win, you set what you get." He said "$2,000." I said, "Get real." We settled on $500 if he won, and he could still stay if he wanted to.

Off to town we went. We bought a basketball and went to an outside court. After the dust had settled, I had a ranch hand for another two months. When he finally returned home, his folks said they couldn't believe what a different kid he was.

Postscript

Jamie returned to the ranch a few years later and kicked my butt at table tennis. Hardly anyone ever does that.

Adolescence, the Myth

Two hundred years ago, childhood ended very early. Children were needed by the family, and for most families, the modern idea of adolescence was a luxury they could not afford. Many a thirteen-year-old boy worked alongside his father or even became the breadwinner in place of his father, who might have been injured or passed away. Children grew up with responsibility, and were expected to assume an adult-like role as soon as possible.

Yes, we all go through a somewhat difficult stage during our years of maturing, both mentally and physically. We all feel awkward and even somewhat rebellious in our search for ourselves, but we don't need anyone pointing it out or using it as an excuse for bad behavior. These rebellious feelings should be regarded as inappropriate, and something we need to keep under control, rather than allowed or even encouraged.

We in the 21th century, and in particular in the United States, have always wanted to give our children all we could. In wanting to make their life easier, we have actually done them harm. We have provided them with so much free time they do not know how to handle it. We have allowed them to do things they shouldn't, say things that should be unacceptable, and given them the excuse of adolescence. We as a society say they are just going through a difficult stage of development and self-discovery; and rebellion and bad manners are just a temporary condition in this developmental stage. HOGWASH! What is unacceptable from a child and from an adult is also unacceptable from a teenager.

I went from being an eleven-year-old boy playing in the sandbox to a twelve-year-old boy who was expected to work after school, and work 40 hours a week during the summer. If I was not playing sports, hunting, fishing, camping, or doing something else deemed important, I worked. As a result, I was comfortable with adults, probably more than with childish teenagers. I thought of myself as an adult from about age thirteen on. I never could understand kids who hated adults, nor acting the way they did, not only towards adults, but each other.

With my teenage sons, I did not go to the extremes my father went to with me. But I tried to make sure they were not overwhelmed by free time. I required them to do a lot of work on the farm or around the house, and I even helped them get outside jobs.

They were not allowed to sleep in except on special occasions, and they were not allowed to lie around and do nothing. They knew if they did not have plans of some sort, their mother or father would find something for them to do.

A child should understand he has a responsibility to the family, and he should be required to contribute in some manner without any compensation other than being a family member. This contribution will help give him pride in himself and in his family. He should certainly keep his room clean, do the dishes, perhaps help with the laundry, and other house cleaning chores. These are not things just for girls and women. A parent does not help a child by doing all the cooking and all the dishes; parents help their child most by making him do his part or even more.

Even those living in a suburb or city can find things to keep their children busy. If nothing else, have them make little rocks out of big rocks. I am serious! A child needs to find something to keep himself active, even if a parent obviously has to invent something. It could be cleaning, painting, repairing, tending to the lawn or garden, or it could be sorting papers, or doing some other chore. If a child is allowed to get out of most of these mundane chores by playing sports or keeping active in an area of their choice, they will find something to do.

Parents need to make sure their son is not hanging out on a corner or at someone else's home. While It might be okay to be at someone else's home or at home playing monopoly or table tennis, lying around talking or watching TV is not okay. They will get enough of that despite their parents' best efforts. Yes, this will require a lot of vigilance on the parents part, but that's their job. The best thing a parent can do is to help their child find a job of some sort. This will bolster self-esteem and help him begin to develop a good work ethic. If nothing else, a job can be invented. A child can be told to go through magazines at the library to find certain types of articles, and to copy them. A parent can invent anything else they can think of, or help him get started in some sort of hobby or sport. Sports and hobbies can be fun, and can even lead to one's life's work. He should be praised and encouraged for what he is doing. Parents should take an interest and help him in whatever manner they can and allow him to get out of some (but not all) of his other chores if he needs more time for his hobby or sport.

If they have taken on the hard tasks with their young boy, their job will be much easier when he becomes a teen. If parents have done very little of the necessary work required prior to their child's teenage years, they will now certainly suffer—and so will their child.

If parents have never required their son to take on responsibility or never required him to respect them and other adults, then parents are almost certainly not going to be able to require him to begin those things now, while he is at this challenging stage of his life.

Handling and giving guidance to a teenager starts well before he becomes a teen. It starts when he is one or two years old and continues right on up to and through his years of so-called adolescence.

A Legend

a poem by Gary Friendshuh

Some time ago, a remembered year,
A new life did appear.
From it rose a Legend true;
A Legend felt at least by two.

A friendship young and ever near,
Love and trust were always clear.
Twas with years, that slight hills grew;
But each one climbed, built love anew.

Then came a mountain, to be alone was right!
To challenge all things, and to test one's might.
Yet on this mountain, this mountain of strife,
Was nature's hand, and a way of life.

To love God's gifts and nature's ways,
Were part of each, through all their days.
So each autumn, of every year,
Two together would draw near.

A field afar, a quarry true.
To match one's skills, and wisdom too,
Always pushing with an inner pride,
And all endured side by side.

Together again and yet alone,
Hear them saying in a silent tone.
A Legend I am, at least to one.
This is my father. This is my son!

My Teenager,
My Friend

I need to say—a father must first and foremost be a father, even if it makes their child dislike them at times. If a father takes that responsibility seriously, as an adult their child will be their friend.

When my boys were still living under my roof, I was first and foremost a father but I liked thinking of them as friends. I later found out the feeling was not mutual with at least one son. After he became an adult, he told me during his last two years of high school he actually felt like he hated me. He also said that with any other father he knows he would have made some really bad decisions during those years.

I do not remember any monumental moment when my boys became teenagers, other than one day they had a birthday and were now 13 instead of 12. It was truly a transformation that went unnoticed.

All the things we had taught them as young children grew with years. Truth, respect, responsibility, self-esteem, a good work ethic, and communication all grew as our sons grew. By the time they became teenagers, truth was a way of life; and they respected their parents and other adults. They had small responsibilities as young children, and now they had more responsibility as older children. By their teenage years, they certainly had healthy self-esteem, and were in the habit of communicating openly with their parents. It just stands to reason that by the time they were teenagers, they were well prepared to handle any physical, emotional, or outside influences.

Yes, there was the question, "Why can't we do it when all our friends are doing it?" but they respected and accepted what, for them, had always been normal. The first noticeable change was when they first acquired their driver's licenses. There, too, we had laid out the rules and what we expected. They knew if they ever got a ticket, they could lose their driving privileges. They also had it drummed into their heads that having a beer was one thing; but driving after having a beer was totally unacceptable and would result in them not driving again as teenagers.

Ultimatums like that can only work if parents are prepared to follow through with them. For instance, a child cannot be told if he doesn't do something, he cannot go along on a family vacation. If parents are not actually prepared to leave him home, they should not make such a threat. Otherwise, their child will soon learn the threats mean nothing.

Because we were very careful in that regard, our sons believed what we told them. If we made a threat, our sons knew it was real. I certainly did not condone my teenage boys drinking beer, other than with me, and I hoped they would not drink alone or with friends. But I had to assume, without letting them know it, it would probably happen at some time. I had to be particularly careful not to set impossible expectations. No matter how good a boy is, he will make mistakes. So rather than setting what I believed to be an unattainable goal or rule, such as you are never allowed to have a beer, I settled for what I felt was more important and obtainable — "If you ever have a beer, you absolutely never get behind the wheel."

I relate raising teenagers to something like the Cuban missile crisis. I did not put our teenagers into a situation they could not retreat from or which allowed them no flexibility. At this age, I had to make sure I did not damage the open lines of communication or inhibit their ability to remain truthful. No matter how good a child he is and how well equipped he is to handle the physical and emotional changes going on within him, there will be times when it will be difficult for him. If he did not want to talk to me at a certain time or about a certain subject, I gave him his space. I did not ask him unending questions about any and every situation.

I talked to him, yes, but avoided asking him questions which may have been difficult for him to answer. I did not tempt him to tell an untruth by continually putting him on the spot. I tried to allow him some flexibility when I did ask him a question. For example, I may have asked if he went to the show last night, and when he answered yes, I dropped it right there. Maybe he went to the show and somewhere else I would have preferred he not go, but I allowed him some flexibility. Then when I got to a very important issue for which I absolutely had to have a truthful answer, I could put him on the spot, and knew he would most likely handle it in a truthful way. If I was going to put him on the spot, I prepared him for it, and allowed him time to think before he answered.

Our human nature, in the pressure of a moment, may cause any of us to respond in a defensive manner that perhaps is not altogether truthful. I was very careful not to put my teenager in that type of situation. I could not condone some of the things most teenagers do, yet I could allow enough leeway so some of the harmless things could be done without having to have him lie to me, or to go directly against what I have told him.

When I was a teenager and camping out, I not only smoked a cigarette (once -yuck!), but we woke people up in the middle of the night by deliberately making loud noises. On one particular night, we even set off fireworks over a police station! None of these things are things a parent could condone or approve of their son doing. Yet, no property was damaged, and very little harm was done. It was kind of being bad without really being bad. I made sure my boys had enough flexibility to be able to do foolish things without my approval, and yet without having to lie or go against my direct orders. I certainly could have told my boys that, when they went camping, they were not to leave the woods or camp site; but by not saying that, it allowed them the flexibility to be a little bad without having defied their father's instructions.

During the teenage years, a parent can certainly help reinforce a good work ethic in their son. As I have recommended before, even if a parent must invent a job, their son does need one. As important as installing a good work ethic is, keeping a child busy and even somewhat tired is even more important. A parent is very fortunate indeed if they can put their son to work or know someone who will. My boys were motivated to work because that was the only way for them to get any money. Even when they were very young, we did not give them even a nickel or dime if they asked for it. Rather, I would lend them money and they would have to do some job to earn it back. By never giving our boys money, they were motivated to want to work so they could earn it. I always told my sons that any money they made would be theirs to spend as they saw fit. When they started making a lot of money, they agreed to put part of it in a savings account, because I had gotten them their jobs.

I encouraged my son to buy (or not buy) certain things by offering either to match the money he put in or by selling him something at less than cost, but ultimately, I allowed the decision to be his.

My father taught me this. When I was 15 years old, in 1958, I was making $100 a week, and had saved enough to buy a motorcycle. My father had a brand new 1958 Ford. As I did with my boys, my dad also allowed me to spend the money I earned any way I wanted. But he wisely did not want me to have a motorcycle, so he made me a deal. If I returned the $750 motorcycle, he would sell me his brand new car for the same $750, but I had to promise I would never buy a motorcycle again while I was living under his roof. I jumped at the deal!

My sons also bought their own first car by pitching in together. I influenced what car they bought by saying if they bought such-and-such a car, I would pay the car insurance.

Try as I might though, each boy had his own personality with regard to money. Luke was a miser and seemed to save it just for the sake of saving it. Tim was kind of average, and Matt could never save a dollar. Anytime he saw something he wanted, if he had the money for it, he bought it. Mark tended to be the most adult when it came to handling money; he always seemed to have it all together. Once again, we recognized that each of our sons were unique, and we allowed them the freedom to be themselves.

For a couple of years, when my three older boys were in high school and Mark was 11, we owned an athletic club. The boys were required to get up every morning before school and clean the club. I kept track of their hours and paid them very generously, but the money went towards paying the tuition to the private high school they attended (or in Mark's case, would be attending). This gave them the pride of feeling as though they were paying their own way, and they had the responsibility of a job.

If a single parent or if both parents are working, their son should understand they need to help at home. His job might be to do the laundry, scrub the floors, or help in some other manner. I recommend not paying him an allowance, but rather paying him by the hour. When I paid my sons by the hour, they were required to fill out a card telling me what they did and how much time they put in on each project. Actually, they were much better at working than they were at keeping track of their timecards. But they did not get paid without the timecards, so this taught them a valuable lesson in responsibility.

Most parents feel a need to give spending money to their children. If parents feel that way, why not create a job so their son can earn it, rather than being given it? Parents need to control their desire to give their children everything possible. They should realize that, in their love and generosity, they can and probably will be causing harm. If instead a son or daughter has to earn what parents would like them to have, they will have something they wanted, and they will have pride in having earned it. As an added benefit, this will free up some of their parents time, and allow them to be more rested and able to be a better parent. They may even have more time to spend having fun with their children. I also feel it is important, and perhaps necessary, that a child be required to have a job in the morning. This job gets him used to getting out of bed and accomplishing something before other children's days even begin. This may sound harsh, but a parent will be giving their child a gift he will carry throughout life.

If parents have done all they could in their son's early years, school is unlikely to be a problem, but rather will be a help in their son's teenage years. I told all my boys I was not going to pay anything towards their college education, so they knew they had to be very good students in order to earn scholastic scholarships. Learning should be, and will continue to be, fun if parents encourage and take an interest in their child's studies. By the time my boys became teenagers, they were all very good readers—thanks to our continued interest and limits on TV use. Being a good student, a child with a good work ethic, and healthy self-esteem also makes it much easier for a teenager to avoid being led astray by peers. For my sons, all the foundations were in place to allow them to handle most any situation, even prior to starting high school and their teenage years.

When raising my oldest three sons, I felt like we were friends, but they were actually closer to each other than to their father. What better best friends can a child have than their own siblings, children that have the same values and upbringing as themselves? I do think if parents pay the price and put in the effort, their children will be friends with each other.

When my fourth son was a sophomore in high school, my wife of 24 years walked away. We believed he should have a choice about who he wanted to live with. We both thought he would choose to live with his mother so he could graduate from the private, all-boys' military school his brothers had graduated from.

He came out to my ranch for his summer vacation, and I told him I was probably going to sail the South Pacific after he left. He told me he'd always felt like it was me and his older three brothers, and him and his mother. He said he wanted to come and live with me, and I owed him that. I said that would be wonderful, but he would have to do more than his part. He would have to be the cook and grocery shopper, along with helping on the ranch. I would be the dishwasher and house cleaner, along with my other normal chores. He said, "No problem."

Mark and I got really close then because we spent a lot of time together. We became the very best of friends, and none of his teenage friends could believe that his father was truly one of his best friends. We worked together, played together, and lived together. We shared our innermost thoughts and feelings and helped each other. I treated him not only as a son and a friend, but actually as an adult. He never betrayed the confidence I put in him.

We only had a serious disagreement once in all those years together. We were driving home and had a mutual agreement that whoever was driving controlled the radio and the temperature. He was driving and had his windows down. I was not feeling well and asked him to roll up the window. When he refused, I pulled rank on him. He stopped the truck, got out, and walked the two miles up the driveway. When he got home, we talked about it. We both apologized, and both grew from the experience.

Mark was a unique teenager, a teenager who was truly an adult. Even his school and teachers recognized this. They allowed him more freedom than they did others, and they accepted his word on things. He was not only a joy for his father, but a joy for his school to have around.

If parents truly work hard at parenting when their children are young, they will find that they will not only take delight in their child's teenage years; but they will have found a new and very good friend.

Throughout this book, I have suggested parents surround any punishment or discipline with lots of love and attention, so a child comes away feeling good about himself. Even though he learns his lessons, he probably won't remember the punishments or discipline.

I realize I have said very little about bumps in the road I had with my teenagers. Perhaps because of all the effort I put into making my sons feel good about themselves, I too feel good about them and have difficulty remembering the trying times.

I did have a couple of uncomfortable moments with my fifth son when he was almost 14. At the time, because I hadn't let things get out of control, the week also contained some special memories. Had I not thought to write these incidents down, to show you I had some difficulty too, I would have soon completely forgotten them.

On a Wednesday, the weather had gotten a little colder. When I was halfway down our three-mile-long driveway, I noticed Daniel was in a tee-shirt. I asked him if he had brought a coat. He said "No." I told him we had enough time to turn around, but he didn't want to. "Dad, I won't get cold," he said. "We only have to wait outside for 10 minutes before they let us into the school."

Had he been younger, this would have been a "my will, not your will" time. He knew I had the right to invoke just that. But because he was almost an adult, and because he was also my friend, I decided to let it slide. I only asked him to promise me he would remember to bring it tomorrow. He did promise, but then he came to the truck the next day without it. I asked, "Where is your jacket?" and he went in and got it. No big deal, but a little stressful.

The other situation was very stressful. We were on

the way home from his football game. They had just won 20 to 14. On the last play of the game, about 30 seconds remained on the clock, and the ball was on the 50-yard line.

Daniel's team ran a running play up the middle. As the back was being tackled, he pitched the ball back to the quarterback, who caught it and ran for another 10 yards.

I told Daniel "nice game." I also told him if I had been the coach, I would have chewed out the back, because the only way your team could have lost was to have a fumble picked up by the other team and run in for a score. Daniel got upset with me. He said they were just having fun. I said it wouldn't have been fun for the rest of the team if the quarterback had fumbled the pitch, and the other team had picked it up and scored.

I was right. That would have been the only way the team could have lost the game. It had been a bonehead mistake, and I wanted my son to understand it. This was not 5th or 6th grade football, this was 9th grade ball, and at this age, they were supposed to be learning how to play the game.

Then Daniel really hurt me. He said, "That's why I like our coach better than you. He lets us have fun." And the look on his face hurt me even more.

He was tired, he was hurt a little from playing, and he was not ready to listen at that moment. I was upset, a little hurt, and maybe even a little angry, but I let it lie. We didn't say another word to each other the rest of the way home.

We are all human, we all make mistakes, and we

all have emotions. I strongly believe we adults need to be in better control of our emotions than we can expect children to be. Most of the time, when a father and a son cannot get along, it is not the son's fault; it is more likely the father's fault. The above situation could have easily gotten out of hand, and to what purpose? To prove I was right? To teach my son about football? To let him know he couldn't get angry at me?

By letting it lie, I was rewarded much more. Later that weekend, Daniel talked to me for over half an hour about some very personal stuff. He asked for my advice, he listened, and he was once again my good friend.

Had I not written down these uncomfortable moments, I would have absolutely forgotten them, and remembered only the very special moment of having my son confide in me.

Mark and the Rocks

Mark and I started our work day at 5am so we could be done by two in the afternoon. We did all the usual ranch things, like tear down old fences, build new fences, check water and cows, move cows, dig water bars, build corrals and sheds, and the like. We worked hard together, and we played hard together.

The ranch was seven miles long, and the only way you could access the west side was by driving 15 miles around, usually through town. That trip took us right by what we called "The Rocks." The Rocks were a series of waterfalls, rapids, and whirlpools. The highest waterfalls was about 15 or 20 feet high. You could dive off a cliff into the raging water below the falls, or you could shoot the rapids, or dive into the whirlpool. It was said the whirlpool had no bottom, but Mark and I dove to the bottom, which was only about 35 feet down.

Below the lower falls was a chute about 100 feet long and only six feet wide. The current was very strong through the chute, which ended at another little falls. Mark and I discovered if you dove to the bottom of the chute, about eight feet down, the current was almost equally strong going the opposite direction.

When we took someone new to the Rocks, invariably one of us would dive into the water at the end of the shoot. The diver would dive to the bottom, swim, and be sucked upstream under the little falls. There, he could sit unseen. Our guest could see no one could have gone down stream unseen, and no one ever believed anyone could go up stream against that raging current—so where did he go? After an appropriate interlude, depending upon the nervousness of any given observer, the other of us would say, "I had better go in after him."

Then the second person would dive into the water and disappear. We never made them wait very long before we shot out from under the upper falls, and were flushed down the chute to the place we had dove in. Just a couple of kids having a little harmless fun (smile).

After our swim, we would lie on the rocks in the sun, then stop to have one frosty-cold beer on the way home and play liar's poker. I had to win two to each one of Mark's, and with that formula, we stayed almost dead even. After our beer break, about 20 minutes or so, we headed back to the ranch. Mark cooked dinner, and I did the dishes. After dinner, we played cards or a game, or just read or talked.

A father and his teenage son—the best of friends.

Postscript

Mark and I were the best of swimmers, so there was no danger for us. Perhaps playing that kind of joke on someone is not appropriate, but I certainly don't claim to always get it right. South Dakota allows a minor to have a beer if he is with a parent, and I felt, as my father did, that if Mark could do a man's work and was as responsible as a man, he was entitled to a beer if he wanted it. We didn't drink for a buzz. We had one draft beer in a frosted mug on a hot day, because it tasted so good. My friend was entitled to that!

Dating and Relationships

For better or worse, when my three oldest sons were in high school (a junior, sophomore, and a freshman), none of them had ever been on a date. They went to an all-boys' high school, so they didn't have the exposure most other boys get. My wife and I talked about this, and thought we might have made a mistake.

So I had a talk with my three older sons. I told them they had to learn how to react around and together with girls. I told them they were going to make many mistakes, trip over their tongues, and be very nervous. It is a learning process all of us go through, but it is a necessary process that should not be put off too long. I have stated before I do not believe this process should start before high school; but as I told my sons, you can't really wait until college, either. A college girl is not going to take too kindly to high school type mistakes when it comes to dealing with a boyfriend.

Having said all that, I asked the boys if there was a dance going on at the school that Friday night. There was. I told them they were going, and if they wanted to sit in the car in the parking lot, that was up to them, but I did not want them home before midnight.

Wow, did we ever regret that! Before that eventful evening, my sons still liked country western music; After that eventful evening the boys told us they had to first endure, and then later began to like, modern rock and roll.

Not only was that the beginning of music around the house my wife and I couldn't stand, now we had to constantly remind the boys to be home on time. Overall, they were quite good at keeping their hours, and only once did one of them go way overboard. He was grounded for a month.

When our sons started dating, we tried to make sure they didn't get into a situation they could not handle. We made sure we knew who they were going out with and encouraged or required them to only double date. We knew where they were going and had a specific time they were required to be home. We never allowed any of our sons to visit a girl who was babysitting, or allowed any of them to be alone in a home with a girl (an adult had to be there).

Another rule came into play about this time. The boys were not allowed to talk on the telephone any more than ten minutes per hour. This again is something that parents will have to determine, but keep in mind that a little unfamiliarity with girls can be a good thing. This phone rule may even make it easier for a child to avoid being rude or trapped on the phone. He can blame his short phone calls on the rules.

Even though a boy may want to show a girlfriend some things in his bedroom, I believe bedrooms should be off limits. Perhaps he could take her in there with a parent, or with one right outside of the door to show her something; but it should never be appropriate for them to close the door to visit (or anything else). This probably sounds prudish; but believe me, when the teenage hormones are raging, parents should not let their son get into any situation that could get out of hand. They should help him, even though he will not want or appreciate their help.

Bedrooms need to be guarded; and even when we were home, we made sure we knew the whereabouts of our son if a girl was visiting. One time when I was in about 7th grade, some friends of my parents came to visit with their 7th grade daughter. All the parents were downstairs, and somehow we wound up in the upstairs bedroom. She lay down on the bed and said I could take her shorts off if I wanted. I can't tell you how my hormones were racing at that moment. Fortunately, I was a little unfamiliar with girls, and too nervous to do anything. We should have never been allowed to get ourselves into that situation.

Now is when some of the groundwork parents laid will bear fruit. If the lines of communication have been kept open between them and their son, they should show an interest each time he does something with his friends. If he has a true comfort zone with his parents, he may even ask them some embarrassing questions about how to act or react to the opposite sex.

Now is also the age when overnight visits can become a serious problem. No matter how confident a parent may be that their children will normally follow all their rules when they are away from home and out from under any immediate supervision, even the best children can be coaxed by other kids to do things they might not ordinarily do. So here too, if parents already have a "no overnight" policy established, then continuing that is easy.

All the effort parents put into their child's younger years will be rewarded a hundredfold. Not only will their job be much easier during their children's teenage years, but instead of being years of worry and full of conflict, those years can be unbelievably rewarding and joyful. If a parent's son or daughter can talk to them about their innermost feelings, this allows the parents to experience their child's joys, fears, and experiences. It also allows the parent to be there and help if they need it. This close relationship with a child is very gratifying for both the parents and the child.

Most parents suffer and dread their son's teenage years. If they pay the price in the preteen years, the teen years, including dating, can be full of joy and wonder for both them and their son.

Even though I had great communication with my three oldest sons, none of them really ever asked about their first kiss, parking, or necking. I would not have minded being consulted about the subject but I did not feel slighted because they never brought it up. When my sons became young adults, however, they did talk to me more about feelings and personal relationships with girls.

While they were still living at home, I talked a little about premarital sex with the older three boys. But my fourth son, Mark, and I were living together (just the two of us), and we became so close and such good friends we did discuss this several times.

What I told Mark was when you make love with a

woman, you take her heart and soul into your hands and she takes yours into hers. You assume a great responsibility, and it should not be taken lightly. It is never okay to just have a good time and use her, or allow her to use you. This is one of the greatest gifts God has given a man and a woman, and it truly is a blessing within a marriage. If you are able to save this special gift for your future wife, then you truly are special. If you fail, make sure that it is what you perceive as love. Most importantly, do not ever take the chance of bringing a life into this world who would not have a mother and father together.

All of us have our own religious and moral values here, and parents all need to decide what is appropriate to discuss and what moral values to pass on. For that reason, I strongly believe parents and family should be responsible for teaching these things.

For the same reasons, any discussions on gender should be with only the parents. (I can't believe I even need to talk about this.) As a parent, I feel a child shouldn't have to worry about gender choice. Until he becomes an adult, I would just tell him he is what he is, and that would be that. I would have protected him for eighteen years.

Hopefully, when he is making his own choices, he will use the values and reasoning abilities his family taught him.

Parents should give their children good moral values and try as best they can to help them associate with families with good values.

If any of my friends ever got anywhere with a girl, they kept it to themselves. They were probably ashamed of not being honorable, and they certainly wouldn't brag about it. Besides, most everyone I knew always went on double dates. Today most of that has changed.

Back then, good values were mostly reinforced by the entertainment we saw. The heroes were the good guys. The good guys told the truth, and they were men and women of high values and honor.

Parents can instill these values into young children before they are exposed to any culture portraying immorality as cool. Then those children will be less likely to be adversely affected by all that crap.

As I have said before, whatever a child learns in his first five years, whether taught intentionally or picked up on his own, will stay with him forever.

The Double Date

This is a true story about how many things can work together to help a teen through a tough situation.

Even though in certain ways I was quite unfamiliar with girls, I had learned to meet them easily.

When I was about 17, I was in a drug store having a soda, and the seventeen-year-old girl waiting on me was a knockout. Before I left, I had her name and her phone number. When I asked her if she wanted to go to the lake with a couple of my friends and to take in a movie afterwards, she readily accepted. We had a fine time, I thought we had a real connection. We even parked for a short time after the movie.

We talked on the phone several times afterwards, and she asked me if I wanted to go on an early evening picnic. She said she would bring the food, and that I was to bring the blanket.

I called my best friend and told him to call his girlfriend because we were going on a picnic.

When I walked to the door to pick up my date, she was all happy, bubbly, and even had a seductive look in her eye. When we got back to the car and she saw we were not alone, she looked like I'd hit her with a ton of bricks.

The picnic was not much of a success, because she was upset all night. She never went out with me again. I found out later she supposedly slept with most of her dates, and no way was she going to go out with a cold fish again.

I am afraid if we had gone on that picnic alone and she had come on to me, I probably wouldn't have had the strength to say no. I was lucky, but my habit of double dating also helped me out.

College

The more knowledge anyone has, the more they want to learn. Give a child a sense of wonder and the gift of knowledge, and he will have truly been given a gift for a lifetime.

But knowledge is acquired in many ways and places. My father was born in 1920. He only went to school through part of the ninth grade, but he became a successful businessman. Though he never placed much stock in a formal education, he was a very knowledgeable man. He could fix or build anything, and he had lots of business sense.

I went to part of one year of college, and I too became a successful businessman; yet I do understand the value of a good education, particularly if you enjoy learning. I believe in today's world, a high school education is an absolute necessity. I do not believe a college education falls into that category.

The most important thing for a child is to be happy in this life. The person who can do what they truly enjoy and make money at it is truly blessed. There are many avenues to financial success. College is one path, but not the only one. A person may be more inclined to work with their hands or in a trade of some sort. Within that trade or within whatever line of work a child chooses to pursue, they can find opportunities to start their own business or create their own business opportunities. Just because they are a carpenter and love what they are doing does not relegate them to pounding nails for someone else for the rest of their lives. If a child has been taught responsibility, given a good work ethic, and healthy self-esteem, he will be able to make enough money in this life to be happy.

I thought nothing of taking my sons out of school to experience life in some other manner. But because they were good students and liked school, they had the opportunity to continue their education after high school. Four of my five sons did just that, and all seem happy in their chosen fields. Matt went to three semesters of college and decided he did not want to stay there. He pursued other interests, and by the age of thirty, was financially more successful than his college-educated brothers.

It's worth repeating. A college education is not the most important factor in financial success. A child's values, work ethic, ability to handle responsibility, and high self esteem will make him successful in whatever he chooses to do. He will not get these things from school. He must get them from his parents.

A Special Memory for an Old Man

When I took my fourth son to college, I noticed a ping pong table in the rec center. We moved him into his dorm room, then went back to visit a little. Soon we were on the table playing a little ping pong. An Asian student noticed us and asked to join. Table tennis is a popular sport in Asia, and he was a very good player. After playing Mark, he and I started playing and he turned it up a level or two. He had me moving all over chasing balls. After several volleys, a group of students gathered around Mark starting laughing.

I asked Mark what was going on. He said they didn't believe I was his father. A brother maybe but no way his father.

It sure wasn't my looks, it was likely because of the way I moved. I think in part that came from trying to keep up with my sons.

Do's and Don'ts

Advice from a father raising his
children the old-fashioned way

Do remember it is your responsibility to teach your child, and give him your time.

DON'T believe the things money can buy could ever replace the most valuable thing you can give your children—your time!

Do give your child truth, respect, responsibility, self-esteem, and a good work ethic.

DON'T leave these things to be taught by others. It is your responsibility. Don't rely on others to do what you should be doing.

Do show your love for your child and for your spouse in front of your children.

DON'T contradict your spouse or argue with them in front of the children. Children need the security of love and family; they don't need to deal with their parent's disagreements.

Do teach your child to be truthful.

Don't lie to your child or in front of your child if you expect him to be truthful with you.

Do discipline your child, and know that TLTs or spankings are sometimes appropriate. Do this at a very young age and when he gets older, you will find much less reason to have to discipline or give TLTs or spankings.

Don't ever hit your child in anger or with a closed fist or on the face or head. All TLTs and spankings should be on the butt or on the hands.

Do always follow any form of discipline—TLTs, spankings, or words—with lots and lots of love, hugs, and reassurance. **Always** allow him to feel good about himself even though he has made a mistake.

Don't dwell on his mistakes but rather praise him for being who he is and tell him you know he will do better next time.

Do always win your battles or confrontations with your very young children. The younger your child is, the more easily these confrontations can be won.

Don't ever choose a battle you do not feel you can win, or walk away letting your child win. You must remain in control. Once control is lost, it is very difficult to recover.

Do teach your young child he must obey his parents and others in authority.

Don't try to be the nice guy and talk him into doing what he is told to do. You all will suffer greatly during his teenage years.

Do recognize your child's special uniqueness and treat him as a human being deserving of your acknowledgment and respect.

Don't ever treat your child like he is not there, or treat him like he does not matter.

Do talk to your child often, tell him stories, or visit with him so he knows you care. Keep the lines of communication always open.

Don't ever be too busy to listen or answer your child's questions. If you do not listen now, he will not talk later when you want him to.

Do support others in authority, even when you disagree with their methods or conclusions. Unless they go against your personal beliefs, children should learn to respect authority.

Don't belittle authority or take your child's side over that of a good person in authority. You may still give your child support and yet show respect for reasonable authority.

Do give your child the comfort derived from feeling as though there is a God who cares for him.

Don't deny your child the right to choose God or religion because you gave him neither.

Do allow your child to love their other parent, even if you are divorced or are no longer in love with that spouse.

Don't ever talk negatively about your child's other parent, even if they talk negatively to your children about you. In time, your child will bless you for this gift.

Do the best you can to recognize your responsibility to your children and then take on that responsibility

Don't worry about your mistakes. You will certainly make them, so just resolve to learn from them.

Do make your child take baths.

Don't make your wife take a bath outside in a horse tank!

Bath Time

When we moved to Colorado, we were on a remote ranch about 10 miles from our nearest year-round neighbor. We had no electricity and no plumbing.

Almost the first thing I did was run a pipeline from a spring down to the cabin.

We then had fresh spring water right at our doorstep. I purchased a propane bottle, a propane hot water heater, and a horse tank.

The cabin only had five rooms (a kitchen, a living room, and three very small bedrooms), so the heater and the horse tank were kept outside.

For privacy, mom would take her bath just before dark when we had all come in from working on the ranch.

If you were male in this family, and if you were lucky enough to have it be your turn, you got the second bath. Mom always got the first. Often, if you were in 5th or 6th position, you were allowed to skip your bath altogether.

Then someone got the idea that mom could take her bath in the middle of the day. That way we would have time to get two tanks of hot water heated, and then we males would never have to take any lower than "third bath.". We assured mom of her privacy by always staying away when we knew she was in the tub.

That worked for a while until the second time a neighboring cowboy came riding over the hill when mom was taking her bath. None of us were even close by (you know, that privacy thing), and the cowboy rode right up to her sitting in the tub.

"Howdy ma'am," he politely said as he tipped his hat.

Lucky for me, the horse tank was full of soap bubbles, and was three feet deep.

We could never figure out how we went for two months having only two cowboy visitors, and both times were when mom was in the tub. (I certainly didn't mention a little modern invention called binoculars. Hey! I was in enough trouble already.)

Needless to say, the tub got moved into the cabin. I built two narrow bunk beds, and the four boys had to share an 8-foot-by-8-foot bedroom.

At night, we ran the generator for an hour or two, and whenever we could get reception, the family all listened to "Mystery Theater" on the radio. The cabin was small enough you could hear it, even if you were lucky enough to be in the tub.

Front to back: Matt, Mark, Tim

Letting Go

Most, if not all parents love their children beyond all telling, and would even lay their life down for them, but a parent's first allegiance should be to their spouse. When children are older, they should sense that their parents feel that way about each other. As close as I was to my boys and as much as I loved them, I knew I was raising them for someone else.

We did not allow them to cut the cord at too young an age, and in the case of Christmas, for example, we let everyone know this is a family time. But when our sons were over 18 and would rather be somewhere else, we did our best to accept it instead of feeling saddened or hurt.

I will never forget the first time our boys obviously wanted to be somewhere else on Christmas Eve. It really saddened my wife. I tried to hug and console her by saying it was just a normal stage, and they would one day come home again.

On that particular Christmas Eve, our boys spent the early evening with us, but then wanted to go their own way. All three of the older boys were out of high school, and I thought it was nice they gave us their time on Christmas Eve. Yet, we had all been so close, so it was still hard on my wife.

Now, fifteen years later, perhaps partly because we did not get angry or try to stop or influence them, they have truly come home.

When I was not invited to a get-together my four older sons were having, I was a little hurt. One of my boys said he felt like he was the moon and I was the earth. He needed to go out on his own, become his own planet with his own moon, and then one day he could come back and truly feel like my equal. I dealt with my disappointment, and now once again I am usually invited when the four or five boys get together.

I believe when a child graduates from high school or turns 18, whichever comes first, a parent can only give him advice and can no longer tell him what to do. Now, if he chooses to continue to live in his parents home, that is another matter. Parents can choose to have certain rules and restrictions if their son chooses to remain living at home. I personally felt the only rules and restrictions should be regarding his conduct and his friends' conduct in our home. The fact he is living in my home should not give me the right to tell him he cannot stay out all night or whatever. But it certainly gives me the right to demand certain conduct, and even payment or favors for the privilege of being able to live there.

The normal saying goes something like this—"I didn't think my father knew anything when I was a teenager, but as I grew older, I realized how truly wise he was." This was not the case for me. When I was a teenager, I thought my father knew everything and was perfect. As I grew older, I saw some of my father's faults and failings and realized he was not all wise.

At whatever stage our children see our faults and failings, all we can hope is they can remember what was good, and more importantly, that they can remember we truly tried.

A Going Away Gift

When Mark went to Australia as an exchange student, I pondered for days about what to give him as a going-away gift. Finally, I asked him what he would like.

He said he would like me to put together a book with all the poems and stories I had written throughout my life. Wow!

Well, I did put the book together, and in it I had a poem about each of my sons. Each one that is, except Mark (Daniel wasn't born yet).

His flight was leaving from Phoenix, Arizona, so we flew down and stayed with my mother the night before he left. I laid awake all night trying to write a poem about Mark, but nothing seemed right. Then about four in the morning, it was just there. It was easy. I wrote it out in long hand and added it to the book.

He said his host family and their friends were fascinated by the book, and it made him feel at home. It was a way to take me with him.

I made copies of the book, put them in a leather cover, and gave one to each of my other sons. Somewhere along the line, I misplaced my copy.

For my birthday one year, Matt gave me a leather book with an embossed painting of me on my horse on the cover. All the poems and stories I had given to each of my sons were inside.

By asking for what he did, Mark really had given a gift to me, and now it had come full circle.

Matt added one page in the front of the book.

Dad,

As a young boy, I can recall grasping the meaning of "A Legend" for the first time. I remember you explaining it, and the sparkle in your eye so acutely conveying the sense of how heartfelt it was. Over the years, the rediscovery of your poems and stories has continued to touch and inspire. When I share this collection with my children, it is like opening a window to who you are, and I thank you for that.

Today, I give back to you your own words in the hope that their message will at times provide you with the joy, warmth, and direction that they have given me.

Love, Matt

Daniel, Mark, Matt, Dad, Tim and Luke

Made in the USA
Las Vegas, NV
06 June 2024

90813544R00134